Give Them Goosebumps

Enlivened Speaking

Miroslav Petrovic

www.enlivenedspeakinginstitute.com
www.miroslavp.com

Give Them Goosebumps Enlivened Speaking © Miroslav Petrovic 2022

Miroslav Petrovic is hereby identified as the author of this work.
The moral rights of the author have been asserted.

ISBN: 978-0-6455257-0-0

All rights reserved. No part of this book may be reproduced, stored in a retrieval system or transmitted in any form by any means (electric or mechanical, digital transmission, recording or otherwise) without prior written permission of the author.

Cover Design by Miroslav Petrovic

Cover Image by Bea Maz

All inquiries should be made to info@miroslavp.com

Disclaimer

The advice provided in this publication is general advice only and intended for information purposes. It has been prepared without taking into consideration your specific objectives and situation.

The author makes no guarantees concerning the level of success you may experience by following the advice and strategies contained in this book, and you accept the risk that results will differ for each individual. The testimonials and examples provided in this book show exceptional results, which may not apply to the average reader, and are not intended to represent or guarantee that you will achieve the same or similar results. This publication is meant as a source of valuable information for the reader, however it is not meant as a substitute for direct expert assistance. If such level of assistance is required, the services of a competent professional should be sought.

While every precaution has been taken in the preparation of this book, the author assumes no responsibility for errors or omissions, or for damages resulting from the use of the information contained herein. To the maximum extent permitted by law, the author disclaims all responsibility and liability to any person arising directly or indirectly from any person taking or not taking action based on the information in this publication.

Every effort has been made to trace the ownership of all copyrighted material. If any omission has occurred please bring this to the author's attention so proper acknowledgment can be given in future editions. This book is intended for informational purposes.

About the Author

Miroslav Petrovic is a TedX speaker, teacher and facilitator who has worked with over 5,000 people across the world supporting them to bring their message to the world. He is the founder of the Enlivened Speaking Institute where he teaches speakers how to go beyond didactic delivery to deliver their message in a powerful embodied way that is enlivening and engaging for audiences. Additionally, he has trained multi-national companies and executives with workplace culture and leadership.

Over the past 10 years, Miroslav has had a rich and diverse speaking, teaching and facilitation career. This has spanned spanned the delivery of various subjects from speaking, sales, meditation, yoga and photography across various applications and diverse audiences from conferences and schools to corporate wellness. In 2019 Miroslav completed an academic thesis with Monash University (Australia's leading Education University) on the role of embodied teaching and learning for creating more engagement within teaching dynamics.

His message and 'off the beaten path' approach speaks to thought leaders, future visionaries, progressive educators and transformational leaders who are empowered to move away from traditional speaking/teaching methodologies and embrace a deeper, more conscious way of communicating through mind, body and spirit. He is fascinated by how we can be more fully alive with everything we do and believes that being in connection with our own personal presence is the most important, dynamic relationship we have in life.

This is the Power of Presence.

Free Workbook

Your copy of *Give Them Goosebumps* comes with a complimentary workbook to support you with the confidence and structure to authentically inspire your audiences and leave an impact.

Download it for free at
https://www.enlivenedspeakinginstitute.com/bonus

Contents

About the Author iii

Introduction 1
   Acknowledgements 1
   A Blessing 3
   About This Book 4
   Why Speaking? 5
   Oh… And *The Fear of Speaking* 7
   A Taste… 9

1. The Quiet Stuttering Boy 11
   Waking Up To Find My Mother Crying 11
   The Brink of War 13
   Prep 15
   The Girl With Black Glasses 17
   Can You Even Read? 22
   The Pain Of New Beginnings 24
   Introverted Upbringings 26
   "Meditation" 29

2. Discovering Presence & Following Signs 33
Leaving What Was Safe 33
The First Big Gig 39
The Signs That Kept Coming 43
The Psychic & The Stage 45
The Drug Dealer 49
Training To Speak: Me As A Student 50
Successes & The Institute 53
Losing It All To Find It Again 54
The Students Experience 54

3. The Old-School Style Vs Enlivened Speaking 57
Method #1: The Old-School Method 58
Method #2: Embodied, Enlivened Speaking 62
Engagement As The Norm 65
Enlivened Transmission:
The Fast Way of Learning 67
Academic Research & The Magic of Presence 70
Goosebumps: The Science 72
The Goosebump Formula 75
1. Alignment 77
2. Connection 78
A Little Bonus 79

4. Principle 1A: Cultivating Stage Presence 81
What Is The Stage? 81
The Stage Is Your Power 83
The Unseen Truth 84
Magnification of Words 89
Choosing Presence Over Avoidance 91

5. Principle 1B: Meta-Fear, Vulnerability, Courage & Goosebumps **93**

    Meta-Fear: Using Fear as a Tool for Presence 94
    Fear In Different Cultures 96
    Separating Story From Sensation 99
    Vulnerability Is Not What
    You Think It Is 103

6. Principle 2: Power of Relationship **107**

    Speaking & Life Is All About Relationship 111
    The Golden Triangle:
    3 Key Relationships of Speaking 113
    A Secret Tip: Enticing Content 115
    Entering The Shared Field 117
    From Speaking *At*,
    To Connecting *With* 121

7. Principle 3: Magnetic Sensing, Adaptability & Responsiveness **125**

    Pause & Breathe 131
    Facts to Stories 132
    Story to Personal Relevance 133
    Translate Technical Jargon 134
    Asking Questions 135

8. Falling In Love With The Process **137**

    The Gift of Mastery 139
    The Relationship To Mastery 142

9. What Is Your Message? **147**
   Discovering Your Message 147
   YOU Are The Message 150
   The Next Step 152
   The Enlivened Speaking Institute 154

References **157**

Introduction

Acknowledgements

I would like to acknowledge the traditional custodians of the land on which this book was written, the Bundjalung Nation and their ancestors past, present and emerging.

Additionally, I want to acknowledge all the teachers, saints, sages, mystics, speakers, seers and wise ones that dared to speak, teach and unravel the mysteries of life to others so that we may have access to them today. Without you, none of this would be possible. The great risks many of you took echo into eternity through our words and actions today. For those of you I have met and taught by in the flesh, my gratitude is eternal.

A big thank you goes out to all my students, clients, audience members and listeners who over the years have continually expressed to me how different it was when I spoke/taught compared to what they experienced with others. This is what made me recognise and reflect on what it was that I was doing. I thank you, for showing me my own magic, without you I would be blind.

A deep thank you to my mother Ljubica and my father Zoran for their love, depth of support and continual promptings of *"go study"* throughout my childhood. I did listen, it just took 30 odd years.

My brother Marko for being a companion on the journey, sister Sara and auntie Svetlana for their ongoing support and ridiculous amount of proof reading. My partner Victoria for her devotional support and love throughout the process of launching the Enlivened Speaking Institute.

Without you all none of this would have been possible.

For all those I have not thanked by name, I apologise and know that your presence was just as valuable.

Thank you to all the people who stepped forward and told me they believed in me. Your words came as timely reminders and without your sentiments this work never would have been created. Let us not underestimate the power heartfelt words have to change the course of ones life and may we continue to speak when it counts.

A Blessing

May this book guide you in your life as these teachings have guided me.

May they be a light in the dark, for you to connect to your aliveness and deliver the words and gifts you alone are here to bring.

The world needs your voice as much as it has needed the voices that have come before you.

May you walk in grace and be guided by the space between words.

About This Book

This book is structured in two parts. Firstly, to give you the context in which it was written. That as a stuttering, mute boy it was very unlikely that I was ever going to be an effective communicator, let alone a successful speaker. Since the first version, many readers wrote to me expressing that my story gave them the confidence and trust to truly see that public speaking was possible for them too.

Secondly, my story is followed by valuable insights into how the Enlivened Method of speaking was created and why it is redefining the bar for what is possible through speaking. This is important for understanding the consecutive chapters. After this I will introduce you to the core pillars for speaking in an Enlivened way, which creates unparalleled connection as well as includes personal and students accounts of how the pillars have been applied, so you can bring them into your speaking and teaching. As you will discover, all forms of 'working with groups' are an expression of teaching — speaking, teaching and facilitating are just different forms of it. The more we diversify our speaking the more powerful we become as speakers.

This book is filled with solid experience gained from my life on the stage as a professional and mystical path. By mystical I mean opening the doorway for connecting to the depths of who we are. The spiritual journey is one that will take us to the depths of ourselves. May your speaking guide you as it has guided me.

Why Speaking?

Do you know what billionaire investor Warren Buffet continually cites as his best investment?

That's right. His first public speaking course.[1] *"I proposed to my wife actually during the middle of the course, I got so confident about my abilities,"* Buffett told Forbes.[2]

Public speaking, as you will learn in this book, is not just about giving a good speech. Working with the stage fundamentally holds the power to transform your whole life. To be more confident, have deeper more meaningful relationships and make more money (whether through business or promotion). The value of public speaking may be one of the most valuable skillsets available to employees, as noted by researchers Docan-Morgan and Nelson:

> *"Once you finish your college degree [...] employers want to hire and work with good communicators. In fact they continually report that good communication skills such as public speaking and presentation ability, are the most important and desired qualities a job candidate can possess."*[3] (see for example[4] [5]).

---

1 https://www.cnbc.com/2017/10/04/warren-buffett-says-this-one-investment-supersedes-all-others.html (Last visited 13/7/2021).

2 https://www.forbes.com/sites/randalllane/2017/09/20/warren-buffett-my-greatest-investing-advice-and-the-investments-everyone-should-make/?sh=159a57df593e (Last visited 13/7/2021).

3 Docan-Morgan, T., & Nelson, L. L. (2015). The benefits and necessity of public speaking education. In K. Vaidya (Ed.)

4 O'Hair, D., Stewart, R., & Rubenstein, H. (2010). A Speakers Guidebook: Text and reference (4th ed.). New York: Bedford/St. Martins.

5 Ulinski, M., & O'Callaghan, S. A. (2002). Comparison of MBA students and employers: perceptions of the value of oral communication skills for employment. Journal of Education for Business, 77(4), 193-197.

Oh... And *The Fear of Speaking*

The stage can be a scary place. One of my favourite stories that captures the dichotomy of what the stage can bring up in us goes back to one of America's most decorated combat veterans of WWII, Audie Murphy. Audie was a boy who lied about his age and had his older sister help him falsify his birth certificate to enter the US Army at the tender age of 16. During his time in the army he was promoted to a lieutenant, was the sole surviving officer in which 102/120 of his company were killed, and he single handedly held off a platoon of Nazi tanks while telling his men to retreat. To say he was courageous was an understatement — the man was the embodiment of courage and valour.

Yet when he returned home and was invited to share a few words at an event in his hometown, created to honour his achievements, he said he would rather face a machine-gun nest than do a speech.[6] This, to me, always encapsulated how the fear of public speaking touches us in different ways, it goes underneath our insecurities and rings them from the inside. *But* we can find where speaking becomes a service. Eventually after a difficult time with PTSD (battle fatigue as it was then called), sleeping pill addiction and sleeping with a loaded gun under his pillow Audie recognised that many of his fellow veterans also suffered from this. This was at a time when PTSD was not openly acknowledged and he

---

6   Wise, J. (2009). Extreme Fear: The Science of Your Mind In Danger. Palgrave Macmillan.

made it a mission to advocate and became an avid speaker supporting veterans and pushing congress to support the mentally and physically injured returning from war.

When we recognise speaking is a service to others, our fear becomes an offering to the altar of life. It is how we are being called to serve. We will unpack how to utilise fear in a constructive way when we get to Principle 1B: Metafear. Let me say that out of the hundreds I have worked with there is not a single person that can not get through the fear — and I find that often the clients I have had which are most debilitated by it often have the biggest messages and most powerful words to share. It's like a tap is released and their essence begins to flow through them again.

A Taste…

"Miroslav," said the woman reading my chart, "*you're here to be a speaker.*"

"*Lol,*" I exclaimed smiling. "*What could I possibly speak about? It has all been said before.*" A lengthy pause ensued as I contemplated and then added, "*The great texts and teachers have already said all there is to know.*"

What I came to discover is that most people were not going to look into those texts that made me come alive and sang to my soul. This was to be my life's song — To connect others to the magic of aliveness that has danced through my life and taken me from a quiet stuttering boy to international speaker. And so it began, the path of the speaker. This may be the case for you too — that the areas you have delved into and developed competency, mastery even, are spaces your audience likely has not transversed, and you are here to deliver that world to them.

Some of us know it calls to us.

Others just answer the call.

In the pages that follow you will discover tangible and direct steps to create powerful transformational experiences with your audiences. You will create more impact and leave audiences feeling deeply touched, inspired and ready to take action. It will challenge you and the way you have approached speaking. If you approach this book with an open heart and mind, it may be one of the most beautiful, empowering things you do.

As you read this book, do not just 'skim' it as if reading any old book. As Linda, an early reader of this book reflected afterwards, *"It's not just a book with great information. Miroslav's presence comes through the pages and I had to slow down, breathe and marinate in the words before continuing."*

At times you may want to slow down, feel, breathe, and let the transmission marinate inside you before continuing. Feeling the depth behind the words is far more important than just scrolling through them.

The book and its wisdom arose from my presence and relationship with life, and may it engage you more directly with yours too.

When you read something that is potent for you slow down, breathe, reflect and feel what it touches within you.

1.
The Quiet Stuttering Boy

Waking Up To Find My Mother Crying...

This first story permeates through me like a faded memory.

I awake, coming out of my room, rubbing my eyes. Little Miroslav, no more than 4 years of age. As I come into the living room I find my mother alone, crying. She is sobbing, her eyes red, with a tissues in her hand, she hardly notices me as she is beside herself.

"*What has happened mum?*" I ask while walking up to embrace her.

"*Dad has been called to the army.*" she replied. He had been called into active duty.

This was the end of our world. The family, the home. From this point on everything changed in ways my parents could never have imagined and I was too young to understand. The war had started. Now, as I write these words, it is I who sobs.

The Brink of War

As the war spread through Bosnia in 1992 we had to flee and make our way across the border to Serbia as refugees. Dad was able to join us and we stayed with relatives. It was a tough time for my parents who had no idea where life would take them. There were many failed attempts at obtaining an international Visa to leave Serbia until finally our family was fortunate enough to be accepted to Australia. We came to Australia as refugees, which for many may hold images of detention centres and crowded boats but arriving legally our experience was a lot more normal.

I say coming to Australia was easy, but that's probably because I was five at the time and had no concept of what 'normal' was. When we arrived in Australia we stayed with my grandfather (mum's uncle) in a four bedroom house with three other families and their children who had also just escaped Bosnia. It was basically one family per bedroom. Food shopping was done daily to provide for everyone. We as kids had no toys but instead played games like who would be the first to see the mail dropped into the letterbox. My parents since reflected on how hard it was to be in a position where they had no autonomy to provide for us. I recall a story they told me a few times of an instance where my two year old younger brother saw a bouncy ball at a service station. He wanted to play with it and began began crying asking my parents for it. Unfortunately they did not even have the $2 to purchase it for him and the man they were with refused to buy it. So instead they just held and consoled my brother as he cried. They reflected how debilitating it was to not be able to support their own family.

Eventually they managed to get on their feet, and we moved out with one of the other families. Things for us as a family began to get a lot better from here and this is also when I started school.

Prep

I was naturally shy, quiet and introverted. It might be easier if I show you a picture. My eyes were always downcast, shoulders rolled in, and I looked so cute in my little blue and yellow uniform. I still get flashbacks of memories where my days at school were spent being quiet and walking around the school alone. Other kids could easily approach one another and make friends, but that wasn't me. Unless people came to play with me I would just keep to myself.

I call this part of me *Little Miki*

I was afraid. Afraid of saying the wrong thing. Afraid of getting it wrong. Afraid of being judged. Afraid of stuttering. Because of my reserved and nervous nature and the fact that I hardly knew the language, speaking at school wasn't really an option. So I learnt to be quiet and keep to myself.

The Girl With Black Glasses

Within those first years of school I took to reading English very well early on and loved being immersed in books. Library was my favourite subject and Mrs Kent my favourite teacher. The library building had two floors and in this one particular lesson we were given free time to explore any book we chose, most of the class staying upstairs. I found myself walking away from everyone as was common for me, and retreated downstairs to search for Animalia (A picture book with lots of animals — it was my favourite).

As I found the book and attempted to pull it from the shelf, this girl standing next to me intercepted and threw the book onto the floor.

"What are you doing! You're so pathetic! It's mine, I got it first! You can't have it!" she teased.

I couldn't respond. I remember her towering over me. She was taller, bigger and had long black hair with thick black glasses. I stood there absolutely terrified as tears began to pool in my eyes, unsure whether to let them out or hold them in.

Inevitably I couldn't hold the tears back any longer and started crying. As they poured through me, I felt both vulnerable and afraid. The girl, startled by my reaction, begged me to stop and began offering me the book. But it was too late, I was already overtaken with emotion and didn't want it any more, and not knowing what to do she ran off.

The library teacher, Mrs. Kent came downstairs after someone told her I was crying. She took me over to sit in 'the pit' with her and Slavisa, the only other Serbian-speaking student in the class. The pit was this cushioned area where she would usually read books to us. But this time, it was only the three of us in there with the rest of the class lining up beside the door preparing to go to the next class. I could hear their murmurs around what happened and why I was crying. Meanwhile Mrs Kent had asked Slavisa to translate her questions into Serbian so I could understand.

"*Miki... can you tell me what happened?*" She said in her ever-so-sweet voice. She was my favourite teacher because she was so nice. "*Miki*" is what everyone used to call me. I never actually used my real name until I was well into my mid twenties.

"*Miki... can you tell me what happened?*" No response, I was so deeply in a state of freeze that not even my eyes gave anything away.

I remember thinking to myself, my throat laden and tensing up with grief and fear.. "*I can understand you fine, I don't need a translator.... But I just can't get the words out!*"

"Miki... can you tell me what happened?

Tears still pooling around my eyes. Head downcast. No. I wish I could, but I physically couldn't.

"Мики, можеш ли нам рећи шта се догодило?" translated Slavisa.

Still nothing.

I tried to speak Serbian — nothing again. The words were physically stuck in my throat.

It felt like being caught between the walls of a canyon compressing together upon me. I was unable to make any sound, not even to scream or ask for help. My body was filled with suppressed anger, rage and sadness yet looking from the outside I just looked stuck and sad. Wanting to speak but incapable of saying a word! I was a prisoner in my own body and there was nowhere to go.

I would like to say this feels like a distant memory, but this level of contraction became my normal. I avoided speaking and making eye contact because that meant less people spoke to me. On occasions when I had to speak it would make me stutter which in turn made me feel even more alone, so I just stayed quiet. Although I am not sure at what point the 'stutter' started, my sense is that this particular incident only exasperated what was already there, imprinted from prior experiences.

During these early years in primary school a speech pathologist was commissioned to come and visit me numerous times throughout the year. She taught me breathing exercises to help me manage my anxiety and stuttering. The first few times I just recall being quiet, listening and agreeing with her. I can't really say whether her techniques worked, maybe to a certain degree they did, but it was not a permanent solution. I also had no control over how intense the stuttering would be, and on one occasion when she arrived I happened to be more relaxed and quietly managed to convince her I was fine and it wasn't happening any more. I never saw her again after that. Phew.

Had it actually changed? No. I just didn't like being called out of class and feeling like the odd one out and the other kids thinking I was 'special' in a weird way. The thought of being examined by this woman again was nerve-racking. Even in the depths of my stuttering I wasn't stupid, I had an awareness of what other people would think and the less I stood out the better. I feared judgement and was happy to do anything to avoid it.

Oh, and a funny little piece of trivia about the girl from the story who bullied me. She actually disappeared after the first year of primary school. Some 20 years later though, a client I was coaching called and said,

"Hey Miroslav, I was telling my best friend about you and what you've helped me achieve in my life and she would love to work with you. She says you may know her,... her name is x,... apparently you went to primary school together?"

Lol, I laughed and looked up at the sky. Smiling, I responded... *"Yeah, I remember her well!"*

The great cosmic giggle. It was the girl with black glasses. I worked with her for a few months after that and allowed the karmic cycle between us to come to an end. After a few sessions I brought up the incident all those years ago in the library. She couldn't remember but profusely apologised for any pain she may have caused me. I smiled and told her it was cool and not to worry about it.

She went on to tell me that she had to leave that school because she too was being bullied. Crazy, I know. To quote or paraphrase the teacher Matt Kahn, *"When people treat us or put us down, they are just showing us the way they were treated and could not integrate. They are showing us with their actions the parts of them searching for love."* I can see now the way she treated me was just her own pain being externalised, and I have nothing but compassion for her. Even a sense of gratitude that we were able to come to closure.

It is humorous though, the way life dances through us.

Can You Even Read?

As the years went by in primary school it naturally became expected that we read on our own and the teacher began to assign regularly solo reading time to the class. Whenever this activity was about to happen I was gathered with a small group of 'special kids' who had learning difficulties and we were taken away by the teachers aids. I guess they assumed that, because I couldn't speak properly, I had mental difficulties. So while the rest of the class did their own reading, myself and the other children were taken to a special room on the side.

Here the four of us sat around a table where they would play a cassette tape to us and we would follow along in our books which had been republished with huge fonts. I was too shy to speak out and tell them I could read, so I endured it. I kind of hated it because it felt condescending, yet I also endured it because I was being a *good boy*.

Eventually, as the term went on, they toned down the cassette tape and asked us to begin reading out loud. I still clearly remember the first moment when I read through the book without a problem. The two teachers aids looked at each other with an expression that I could only define as shock and awe as to why they had kept me there for the whole term.

In retrospect I wonder why I did it to myself. Why *I pretended to fit in*, instead of just speaking up. But little

Miroslav didn't have that awareness, courage or the words. The bigger recognition now in retrospect is that self-suppression wasn't a once-off event. I could look back on my life and see numerous times where I had done this — tolerating situations instead of speaking up.

Maybe you've had this experience too? Being nice instead of standing up for something that feels true to you. Those times we refuse to act or speak to what feels alive for us because we are afraid of being judged, outcast, labelled, or changing the social dynamic. Where have you allowed yourself to just "fit in" instead of being true to yourself? How much time and energy have you wasted on these endeavours?

The Pain Of New Beginnings

Both being skilled workers my parents found employment very early on and were able to provide for the family and build a base. They worked hard initially doing jobs which were not in their expertise but they wanted us to be looked after. We had a tight family unit: home, food, holidays, Christmas gifts. All the things that I assumed were predominantly normal in Australian life I now look back on and feel privileged to have been able to receive their love and support in such a way. Despite all this we rarely ever connected in a deep way. It still pains my heart that we could talk so often but never fully understand each other. My parents never really knew who I was — either from my fear to express it, or my inability to do so. My Serbian vocabulary was that of a 5 year old, and although I could do fluent small talk I was never really able to express what truly mattered to me. Life had been tough on my parents migrating over here — they had left their perfect cushioned life to begin life anew, in a foreign country with *nothing*. Their entire focus was on providing stability for my siblings and I for which I have eternal gratitude to their sacrifice. Throughout my adolescence my connection with my parents was one of mutual love and acceptance but never emotional transparency and depth. It was coexistence. My experience is that this story is not just unique to my family, but is the story of many families the world over. We co-exist, sometimes for decades without really connecting. And it shatters ceilings when we do begin expressing ourselves.

There is a good chance that what you learn later in this book will also support you to bridge those family divides.

In my trainings I have seen students reconnect with family members they had not spoken to in years, often resulting in tears and genuine connection sometimes for the first time. All of these parts of expressing ourselves in our private life link back into how we show up on stage as you will learn later.

Introverted Upbringings

My experience of massive introversion lasted all through my schooling and well into my college/university days. It was sometime during university that I got my first taste of meditation. Well, actually, it was a *bit* weirder than that? Shall we go there or should I just *gloss* over it?

I suppose I should tell you a little of the story.

It was around this time when one of my best friends went to an *awakening ceremony*. I had no idea what that meant but he was quite a sceptical guy so I was obviously intrigued. He explained how he went to this ceremony and then viscerally described the feeling of an 'energy' rise through him, from his base and then get stuck in his throat. Fascinating right?

Later that same night I was taken through my dreams into one of the most insane and scary altered state experiences I have ever had. Although the entry to it happened through the dream state, the experience was hyper-real. The dream was originally placed in a pool hall where I was playing pool with some friends. Out of the corner of my eye a woman began to approach me. She was no ordinary woman, looking more like a mythical villain from a Marvel film. She walked right into my personal space and demanded:

"Where is the golden bird?"

Although in any kind of rational state this wouldn't make sense. What golden bird? But in the dream, I KNEW the golden bird was located at the base of my spine. But, I didn't want to tell her. She continued looking directly at me, not breaking her presence for a moment. She was adamant. While continuing to look at me she lifted her right hand and then began screeching at a pitch high enough to shatter glass. The sound filled my whole body and fear flooded through me. There was nothing I could do but surrender to the experience. I let it take me.

As the sound unleashed through me my body felt like it was exploding with a golden light, bursting through my skin. At one point I was so overwhelmed with the bliss moving through me that I felt like my body was levitating. There was more bliss, fear, and awe than is possible to imagine or describe. It was as if I disappeared and all that was left was this sensation. Waves of light and sound vibrating and moving through me. But there was no 'me' anymore, just these exhilarating sensations. I could not feel the edges of my skin or body. It was so overwhelming that the only thing I could do was to surrender, and when I did it was as if this massive screeching sound and light exploded through me. All time disappeared and it felt like I was lost in that moment for ages. Both beautiful and terrifying.

Eventually the visions in the dream settled like dust beginning to rest at the bottom of a glass and I began to feel the bed underneath me, still unsure where my skin stopped and the rest of the room began. I laid there crying for what could have been 20 minutes or 3 hours, but felt timeless. The dream itself was obliterated through the intensity of the experience, only sensations and tears were left, streaming through me as I lay in sweet surrender.

Although I couldn't make any conscious sense of what I had just experienced, I knew one thing for sure. It affirmed my belief that there was more to life than the mundane reality I had grown up in. This spiritual existence was something I wanted in my life.

The following night as I got ready for bed I was both terrified and yearning for more of whatever that experience was.

That single moment had set about a lifelong craving to return to that depth of relationship with life.

"Meditation"

That craving for 'more' was first quenched when I was introduced to meditation. My journey into meditation actually began with a Tantra Yoga Teacher Training. I had never even practised Tantra but found myself insecurely diving head first into a teacher training. The training was based in both neo-tantra partner practises and traditional tantra meditative practises. At the first session the teacher, an older man with long grey hair, demonstrated an exercise and asked us to teach another student in the group. As they all began to partner up, I, being so quiet and insecure, just stood there un-partnered as nobody approached me. Finally the teacher signalled, came over and said, *"You can work with me."* As if my already existing anxiety levels weren't high enough, I now had to work with the teacher.

"Okay..." I replied shyly, as I began to demonstrate the exercise, slowly moving my hands back and forth to illustrate the movement of the breath.

He paused, looked at me curiously and slowly pulled his glasses down his nose peering at me directly over the top of them. He spoke very directly:

"You are a teacher. You are here to speak and bring this work to the world."

Although a part of me wouldn't let myself believe it, another part of me knew the truth of his words. It was as if he had rung the bells of truth at the core of my being — and so it began.

Through my time with Tantra and meditation I began to *feel* again. My anxieties and the walls I had built to protect myself slowly began to come down. For the first time I could recall, I began to feel at home inside my own body. It was intoxicating. I loved every moment of it. As I write this now I can feel the tears welling up at how deeply I appreciated those times spent meditating in my younger years. I would drive for 45 minutes to get to the meditation class, meditate for an hour, then drive 45 minutes back home again. Meditation was the highlight of my week and all I wanted to do.

Sometimes people think that meditation is some technique you learn to do that involves closed eyes and crossed legs, but this is not it. Meditation is about what those techniques connect us to. It is a bit like walking. You learn to walk to get to places, not to rehearse different styles of walking. **Meditation is about having a direct relationship with life,** unbounded by thought. By default we unconsciously objectify reality and then relate to it through the mind without even knowing we are doing this — it is only when the mind slows down, such as in the time after a massage or a deep and meaningful conversation with a friend that we feel more intimately connected to life itself. Meditation is the doorway to creating this within ourselves. It allows us to put thoughts and concepts aside and relate to life directly. Consider it like the difference between Coca-Cola and a cheaper brand of Coke. After you've tasted the real thing, or connected with life directly, the others feel like cheap imitations. But if all you experience for long enough is the cheap imitation, you begin to think it's 'normal' and forget what's truly possible.

Meditation is the doorway which allows us to relate directly and intimately with life.

As I deepened into meditation, it became an increasingly comfortable and familiar place. I enjoyed being that deeply connected to myself and life. Shortly thereafter I began asking the question:

"This is great, but I am stuck with my legs crossed and my eyes closed... How do I experience this level of connection with other people? With my eyes open?"

The answer came quickly. **Speaking, teaching, and facilitating.** Working with groups and creating this depth of connection for and with others.

I did not know it at the time but my early challenges of being so socially awkward and introverted had set me up for the work I was about to do. They had led me to meditation which had allowed me to come out of my own insecurities and to begin to see the invisible world. The pre-verbal world of connection, feeling and rapport which was to be instrumental in the way I was to approach teaching, speaking and facilitating over the years to come.

2.
Discovering Presence & Following Signs

Leaving What Was Safe

By the age of 25 I had been teaching and practicing meditation for about five years. The presence it connected me to had become a foundational part of my diet, my thirst for life.

Around this time I also moved out of the family home for the first time. A month or two into my new self-living adventure I started receiving a recurring message that kept surfacing during my meditation classes.

"Leave your job. Run a cacao event."

At first I thought this was a bit crazy. I was working a pretty easy-going and well-paying job as a photographer and graphic designer. It also gave me a lot of free time to myself. Unfortunately, the message kept coming; I continued to push it to the side, committed to having a safe income now that I was living alone.

This continued for a few weeks until I was hosting one of my meditation classes and had to stop, as I could not contain my laughter.

"What's happening?" One of my students asked, smiling at me.

I laughed and told them I couldn't actually guide the class because all I kept hearing was: *"Miroslav, leave the job and run the event."*

They giggled and I blurted out loud *"Okay, I will do it."*.

Thus began the turning moment.

What happened next was amazing. In the following 6 weeks my business partner, Paras and I amassed a team of about 20 volunteers. We created, marketed and hosted an event with 200+ attendees. It was sponsored by brands such as Pana Chocolate and Loving Earth. This all happened with no prior training in event or people management or marketing. So, how did we do it?

Through speaking. Yes, that old thing. We invited our epic

friends and all the amazing people we knew from different facets in our communities, and told them about what we had envisioned and what we were creating. They said *"yes"*, and magic was born. Goosebumps literally became our barometer. If what we were doing was giving us goosebumps, we knew we were on the right path. It was a relationship with aliveness.

It all came down to speaking. It was not to be a 'once off' thing. I recognised I would have to speak in front of groups to sell the vision and connect with people. I also had to make videos to promote the event online, and to speak at the event to get all the attendees into the experience. It was to become a part of my lifestyle, as it truly is for anyone that's in leadership. Speaking was the lifeline of making the event a reality. Every speaking opportunity, whether you call it a meeting or a zoom call, is an opportunity to enrol people deeper into the vision we are creating as leaders.

How did I do it? How did I go from being terrified of public speaking to creating this level of enrolment and impact? Presence. Meditation taught me that if I could lean back into my presence, the world would open up for me. Instead of planning a talk on how I could inspire people or writing and memorising a script, I would soften into my presence and let it guide me. My mind would go quiet, just like it used to during meditation, and then I would watch and listen to the words move through me. And guess what? The words reached people. *It touched their hearts, because I was opening my heart to them*! Because I wasn't in my head thinking about what to say next, I was able to be present *with* them and they felt it.

At one of our first team meetings, Ruth, a middle-aged woman with a bit more life experience than the rest of us, leaned in to me and said:

"Miroslav, have you noticed what happens when you speak?"

"What?" I replied.

"*It is as if everything goes quiet. My mind just stops and the only thing I hear is your words.*"

"Wow" I thought... "*This whole time I thought this experience was only happening within me!*"

When I speak I often find myself as if in a vacuum, a meditative state. My mind would go silent and I would watch or listen to the words emerge from me.

In that moment I realised that not only was this experience happening within me, but within everyone present. I am eternally grateful to Ruth, and the many others after her who expressed similar sentiments, for without them I never would have recognised my own magic. The implication of her insights is that when we are on stage, as a speaker, whatever is happening with us is also broadcasting and affecting the whole room. So, if a person is nervous, their nervousness is being amplified and affecting all the listeners. Hence, when first timers come on stage to speak, we don't actually remember any of their words, just the level of nervousness. Our feeling state speaks just as loudly as our words.

This event, that I left my stable job for, became known as Tribe One Heartbeat. You could say it was the first NYE party of its kind. No drugs, no alcohol, just people connecting in a fun, authentic heart-centred way. We were featured across Australia through the mainstream media: Channel 9, The Herald Sun, and Sydney Morning Herald. It brought joy and connection to thousands of peoples lives.

At our first big event of over 200 hundred attendees I had to speak during the opening ceremony and bring everyone into a shared presence. I don't remember the talk as much as what came afterwards. Pana, the founder of Pana Chocolate, Australias biggest raw chocolate company and one of our sponsors for the event, came up to me and asked:

"Miroslav, do you feel nervous when you speak?"

I paused.

"No..." I replied, searching for words. *"I'm not nervous about speaking. I just hope that I will be connected to my heart ... and I trust and know that if I have that, everything else will be fine."*

What I called my heart back then, is now just connection. Connection to myself and connection to others. The only way this level of connection can emerge is through *presence*. Presence, is what allows for goosebumps to happen. Presence, is quite literally the container in which all speaking and transformation happens.

The First Big Gig

It was the day of my first big gig. I was invited to speak at an event which was part of a group of global synchronised meditation events. There were going to be hundreds of people in live attendance. At the time I was living in a small two bedroom apartment with a tiny balcony full of plants. The day of the talk it was storming and I spent the entire day outside on our little balcony writing and rewriting my speech as the raindrops teetered around me. I was trying to plan and structure what I wanted to say that evening. It. Did. Not. Work. By the end I was ready to tear my hair out in frustration.

The rainfall around me had created a meditative space where I recognised all my ideas were there on the paper, but it was impossible to 'plan'. Working out the precise order was only doing my head in, not to mention even attempting to memorise the speech. It just became clear that I wasn't going to do it this way. The mental noise and confusion in my mind began to clear in a way only storms can do, the coolness of the air pulling my focus into attention.

I took a few breaths… connected inwards, and leaned back into that presence again.

This was not going to be a perfectly planned talk.

The process was inviting me to let go.

To listen to what wanted to be heard.

To give the talk its own life.

Just as I had done every other time.

To dive into the unknown and let presence carry me.

As the writer Ray Bradbury had exclaimed...

"You've got to jump off the cliff all the time and build your wings on the way down."

I let go of the planning and realised what I needed was already inside me.

I walked into the venue that night. Second Story Studios. It was a unique space, a massive refurbished saw-tooth warehouse in inner Melbourne. The kind of place where trendy companies do their staff events. The front area had a stage and low bean-bag style seating, while the back housed an open-bar with people still milling around.

I went out on stage and gave it 120% of myself.

I disappeared and the days efforts in preparing just poured through me organically.

If you had asked me what I did up there, I would have had

little sense of memory. Many of the words that I spoke that night poured through me for the first time. Ideas and stories come together in brand new ways. My life experience became powerful stories as I encouraged them to follow a path of courage. The MC of the evening, a young woman who was also a radio and sporting presenter, came out and captured it perfectly in a testimonial she wrote for me later:

"Miroslav's ability to engage an audience from the word GO is second to none. His calming tone and grounded presence sets the atmosphere for the 'conversation' — it created a sense of unity where everyone was on the same wavelength by the end of his talk. **Miroslav ignites inspiration within his audience** *— an opening of ideas, one to many and many to one."* — Justine McInerney

It was as though the audience and I had pulled on the invisible threads between us that nobody could see, but the presence of which we could all feel.

Afterwards, a woman from the back of the room came up to me and said, *"I have no idea what you were speaking about but it was magnetic, I felt so drawn to you throughout your whole talk but felt obligated to stay with my friends at the back of the room."*

Her words were a gift that early on showed me something crucial.

Speaking is not just about the words we say.

The words are essentially just the packaging for our message.

What is even more important is the place we are speaking from — What I earlier called the '*felt state.*'

What she was relating to or feeling from the back of the room was my presence. That's what was magnetic.

You could call this the feeling, the essence, or the energy, but to speak *from* this place is where we touch people. It is what's magnetic, alive and creates goosebumps. It's what allows us to *connect.*

And I had just developed an insatiable thirst for more of it.

The Signs That Kept Coming

Between these early achievements and actually building a career out of speaking, teaching and facilitating there was a lot of failure, hardship and depression. There were amazing days, when I got to be on stage and make a good deal of money, but there were also weeks and months where I did not make a single dollar and lived in anxiety over how I would pay my next bills. I felt like a fraud and a failure. On one occasion during this period I repeatedly ran into a man on the street who told me to do a kitchari fast (A mix of rice, lentils and spices). I thought *'Well, why not? I've got very little money left anyway'* and I spent my last $72 to buy two weeks' worth of ingredients to keep me going. Kitchari was all I ate for the two weeks.

During this period of my life I wanted very little, apart from doing the work I was here to do, and thus learnt to live with very little. This struggle went on for close to a decade. I still remember the courage it took to launch my first ever workshop. I meticulously wrote and revised all the details and marketing for hours... only to have it launch and sell no tickets. But I had such massive goosebumps going through the process that I knew this was my path and it was what I came here to do, and the only way was forward. I sacrificed everything to be in deeper relationship to this path. However, throughout this time it's as if there was a lifeline, urging me on, urging me to keep going even when I considered giving up and just routing back to a normal life with a normal job. But I couldn't, there was something deeper calling me.

You may have received some of these signs yourself. Recurring thoughts, repeated words from strangers, symbols in your dreams. Perhaps goosebumps when reading or hearing something highly relevant to you. Some of these signs may have even led you to finding me and this book. Some people speak of it like it is a message from the universe; I see it more as life itself communicating with us. Life showing us the path we had chosen to walk before we had even been born. A more logical-science-y friend of mine sees it as symbols from our unconscious mind about the choices that are in deepest alignment and desire for us to follow. You may have experienced some of these or live by them in your life. Let me share a couple of these through my hardest years that became my guiding grace.

The Psychic & The Stage

Mind-Body-Spirit-Wellness expos ... a place where spirituality enters the mainstream. One year I went with my friend, Jen. She was a doctor and as expected, rather skeptical about a lot of these spiritual-y things. After wandering around the expo with its usual array of spiritual materialism, books, crystals and some other irrelevant 'stuff' like glamour photography we came to rest at the main stage. The seats were already packed as the main act was about to kick off. He was a psychic-medium called Jason McDonald and everyone was amped to see him.

Jason came out and explained that he would start speaking to the spirits he was seeing on the other side and would let us know what they were saying. The next 20-30 minutes he would describe different people holding certain objects or passing certain messages and people in the audience would raise their hand if it was someone they were familiar with. Now, even writing this, a part of my mind remains skeptical, but what I saw in the room was undeniable. The specificity of some of the insights Jason told were uncanny, and it became highly emotional as people cried, hugged and reflected on messages from their loved ones. The room became a sea of goosebumps, and the more messages he delivered the more potent the energy in the room became. Jen gripped my arm stating, *"Miroslav! How is this possible?!?"* I smiled, his words and presence were destroying any sense of skepticism either of us may have had.

We were standing at the back behind all the seats, and by now an even larger crowd had gathered behind us. There were probably a couple hundred people around the stage; everyone fully captivated, waiting to see what would happen next. At this point he looked over to the back of the crowd, staring straight into my eyes. It partially terrified me as I hoped he wouldn't ask me anything... then he declared:

"You will have a massive speaking career, especially in the States. I see the star spangled banner behind you on many stages. You are a powerful creator and can make anything happen; you just have to get rid of what's happening up here." He finished the final sentence while motioning in circles around his head.

As he said it a wave of sadness hit me. I felt both deeply seen, my path acknowledged, and the dreaded weight of the path ahead. I knew his hand waving around the head was referring to my old friend depression. The not wanting to get out of bed in the morning, feeling life is too hard, not wanting to be judged. Although I call it depression, I probably lived this way for a good decade before I ever recognised it for what it truly was. Before then it was just 'normal life.' But he had called my path out into existence from my own mind. From this moment on I knew there was no turning back and the only way was forward.

In the years to come, the vision of me being a speaker was repeated many times in different ways. It was as if the indwelling mist that lived behind the fabric of life was whispering to me saying, "Hey... you... follow this. Your calling is in this. Your fear is in this. Your love is in this. All your greatest desires will come to truth, to fruition, IF you follow this."

So, I did. And over a decade later it is still what I am doing.

In Jason serving his purpose, he delivered the fullness of mine.

As if landing a sword through my heart into the earth.

Declaring: It is time.

Over the years, there have been times I felt a great desire to give up. To throw it all away. To just live a simple life. As a farmer, as a photographer, as an employee. Sadly, or perhaps gratefully, none of it ever worked out. Despite all this, NOTHING ever gave me the same feeling, the same purpose as being on stage, as being with other people. You, dear reader, may have a similar calling, whether you have tasted it yet or not.

I knew speaking is what I was meant for, and there was no turning back. My soul had been awoken by this melody and having heard it was not going back to sleep.

As the great spiritual teacher Muktananda once said, and I paraphrase, "Once the spiritual path has been awoken, there is no turning back, and a seeker will go after it their whole life."

This was it. And it didn't look like meditating in an ashram or living in the Himalayas, but rather serving the world through my speaking, teaching and facilitating. This was my journey home to the depths of myself, and it might be yours too.

The Drug Dealer

I have had countless people tell me of what I am here to do, from calling me a speaker, a teachers teacher, to a prophet. But one of the most memorable was when I got contacted by a man that used to be a bouncer at a bar I visited occasionally when I was younger. He contacted me on social media and told me how he had been having a tough time with drug addiction and was deeply grateful for how everything I had put on social media had helped him over the years. He wanted to take me out to lunch. When we went for lunch he shared insights from his drug binges, where he'd had visions of seeing me on stage and how successful I was going to be.

Crazy.

Sometimes when you want to give up, life backs you in uncanny ways.

Training To Speak: Me As A Student

Although speaking came naturally to me I knew I could learn a lot from those that had gone before me. At first I attended a couple weekend workshop-style basic speaker trainings, until I came across a legitimate program that was only offered once a year. It cost about 6k and I went back three consecutive years. It took going back three times for me to integrate it all. As you can imagine, a full week of speaker training was information overload. For me, at the time, it was a lot of money, and the first time I had invested in myself in this way. The money I invested had been saved up from 10+ years working as a paperboy throughout my childhood that my parents had helped me with. Paperboying was *hard* work that was not well paid. It would take all four of us about 3-5 hours to fold and deliver the papers to the local neighbourhood and often paid less than $50 for the day. (Cumulatively, that would have been about $12 each if we were splitting it, or approximately $3 an hour.) Instead my parents put it into a savings account for me to have when I got older.

Naturally my parents assumed and were entrusting me to put it to good, sensible use, like a house deposit. I knew where life was pulling me though and realised I wanted to invest into this speaking course. I vividly still remember the very hard conversation I had to have with my father. I sat him down on the couch and told him there was something important I wanted to speak to him about.

"Dad," I said, afraid, unable to make eye contact.

"The money we've saved up from paper rounds. Is this my money or yours? Because if it is yours and you want to choose what to do with it I would rather just put it in your account and you choose where you invest it. And if it is mine, I would like to invest it differently and do a program on speaking."

"Son, it is yours, and I entrust you to make the choices that are best for you. I'm here just to support you as best I can."

Bless my father for being so understanding and believing in me because that conversation was a major mile-stone in my life. This conversation itself was just as valuable as the speaker training. It allowed me to reclaim *my* life and step out of living the life I imagined my *parents* desired for me. If my dad had said no, my life probably would have been very different now. To this day I am still grateful as to how he sees the world, and the love and spaciousness he has had for my siblings and I.

Years later after completing these trainings I found myself on the speaking circuit doing a tour of Australia. I was lined up to be the final speaker at a three day event. In that one hour of being on stage I made $7,000. It blew my mind! At the time it did not fit any of my ideas around what was possible. I was used to *working my ass off* for this kind of money, and it was as if the universe had sent me a wave of grace to say, *"Miroslav, this is your path, keep going."*

From that moment on, speaking became something I could lean into. I knew very little about marketing or running a business but I recognised if I put myself on the stage people would want to work with me because of how deeply I was communicating with them. Now I teach others how to do this, regardless of what their message is. The only way we are going to change this planet and our communities for the better is if we reconnect to people's hearts so we can collectively be in a deeper relationship with life.

Words alone are not enough, we must touch people where it matters.

And the only way to touch people is to be in touch with ourselves.

Successes & The Institute

It was probably a decade of ups and downs, successes and lulls to come to a point of stability in my career.

Over the years my work in speaking, teaching and facilitating has taken me many places and in-front of well over 5,000 people. From working with teams inside companies like Lululemon Athletica, to, most notably, speaking on the Tedx stage about overcoming fear and using it as a tool for personal and spiritual evolution. My most fulfilling achievement was the establishment of the Enlivened Speaking Institute. The Institute's mission is to teach people how to speak, teach and facilitate with aliveness — so they can take their message to the world and inspire audiences into heartfelt connection.

The Enlivened Speaking Institute has taken speaking from memorised oration to enlivening experiences that touch the hearts of the audiences. Over the years, students, listeners and audiences at our graduation talks have regularly cited *"I had so many goosebumps watching you all speak!'* Goosebumps, truth and authenticity are the foundation for a fulfilling life as a speaker and as a person.

Losing It All To Find It Again

One of my biggest wins was during the Covid pandemic. It didn't look this way when it first hit us; my income dropped by 95% as everything I was doing up until then was in person. After some months spent in contraction, I ended up launching an online program that made $20,000 without a single dollar spent on advertising. How? The pandemic opened up the massive potential of speaking on digital stages. Other people would invite me to come and present to their communities about Enlivened Speaking, and at the end I would offer my services. People could see and feel the aliveness of how radically different my approach was to the typical monochromatic memorised speaking they were used to.

I would do live demonstrations with a volunteer and show how much more aliveness we could create very quickly with the Enlivened approach. The rest of the audience could see how much more power and engagement their peers could hold with just a couple of tweaks from me. They wanted more and dived in to learn how to speak in this way themselves. Covid became a blessing in disguise, as it forced me to take my work to the next level.

The Students Experience

Since then the Institute has trained over 100 speakers just in its first year. The results have been mind-blowing for students both on and off the stage.

When we genuinely touch people they become open to hearing us and wanting to work with us. One of my clients this year, Miranda Marriott, added $60,000 to her income in just 6 months as a result of the work we did on her speaking. In her case, she utilised purely digital stages during Covid, and even had old leads reach out to her and say, *"I don't know what you're doing, but I can feel you now and want to work with you!"* We will go deeper into the art of creating this experience in chapter six on cultivating relationships with the audience.

Facilitator Andrew Mai recollected how, before doing this work, his patterns were a *"tendency to be in my head overthinking what I'm saying to other people."* He discovered that he was wanting to be liked where as now, the course connected him to a more grounded sense of who he is. He explained how this work impacted the quality of all his relationships, *"My sense of self, not just the way I present on stage but the way I connect with others."* These sentiments are a common experience amongst many of the institute's graduates as you will discover in the chapter on presence.

Another one of my clients Lauren Becker, an intimacy coach,

said that as a result of this work not only did she have more people reaching out to work with her but there was now also a much wider spread of clients coming to her. At the same time this is not the case for everyone. What I truly know is that Enlivened speaking will get you in touch to the next part of your path. For example, Pamela Kirkley, another client of mine went from being a social worker to getting employed as a team leader in another better paid role which she credited to the increased confidence she had received through the course.

This is the power of speaking from this depth — it opens us up to the next stage of our lives.

3.
The Old-School Style Vs Enlivened Speaking

As you can see from my story, my path to speaking was not typical. I never really asked for it, life called me here and I kept leaning into it and saying yes. Speaking to me was a soul or spiritual path as opposed to training for a vocation. I quite literally forged my own path and created a completely different model than what was traditionally out there. It was a product of my life's experience, unique studies and ways I had utilised speaking, teaching and facilitating.

There are two basic approaches to speaking. One is the old-school approach, which is a bottom up approach. The second is my Enlivened Method, which is a top down approach. They both have unique elements and challenges which will suit different types of people. Below I outline the two different models and approaches to speaking.

Method #1: The Old-School Method

The first one you may be familiar with. I call it 'old-school' because it was what many of us were taught in high school and is often dry and tedious. In this model you begin with writing a speech, editing it, rehearsing it, then getting on stage and reciting by memory what you had written. Thus a lot of time is spent on memorising and reciting — without any sense of engagement! It takes a great amount of commitment.

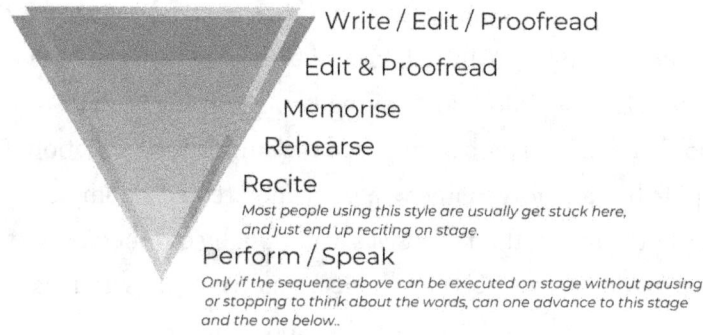

This approach is also often taught by 'business-gurus', who have mastered a sales script for speaking that creates repeatable results and then teach all their students to do the same. It is somewhat a cookie cutter approach and often you can see who a speaker has been instructed by based on the structure of their talk because it is robotic and predictable.

The advantage is obvious, it worked for the guru, it will work for the student too. Because it is simple and they are told specifically what to do it creates a good, repeatable level of performance fairly easily. The problem is that trying to fit into someone else's cookie cutter can often look forced or awkward on you.

There are times when this approach may be favourable for example if you were doing a world tour and wanted to repeat the same talk over and over again, it may make it easier if you had it all memorised. Secondly there are also times when I would highly recommend you lean more towards this type of approach, and that is when every single one of your words has to be precise.

Nelson Mandelas *I Am Prepared To Die* speech is a great example of the old-school approach utilised in the correct way. Mandela was on trial for counts of sabotage, furthering communism and aiding foreign powers which was punishable by death penalty. He and his co-defendants decided that instead of testifying as witnesses and undergoing cross-examination, he would deliver a speech on their behalf from the defendants dock that would put the state on trial. It was a three hour speech and he worked on it for weeks with the help of friends, a journalist, author, and his lawyers. This is not the kind of thing one wants to leave a chance with. The speech ends with the line *"But, My Lord, if it needs to be, it is an ideal for which I am prepared to die."* Witnesses say he delivered this final line looking straight into the eyes of the the judge. His lawyers had advised him to remove it completely as it may provoke the judge to sentence him to death, but instead he added the qualifier *"If it needs to be"* and kept it anyway. Instead he was convicted to life imprisonment, serving 27 years until he became President of South Africa.

In that context, by all means it makes sense to write and memorise when so much factual data is at stake during a judicial hearing. It is not the context many speeches are made in though. In most of the contexts you may find yourself in, reading from a piece of paper in todays modern world will likely be received as boring and overly rehearsed. Writing and memorising can diminish everything that makes a presentation come alive. People often end up disconnected from their audience. This is because they are either reading or in their heads thinking about what line comes next and hoping they don't forget it while trying to do all the things they've been told are 'right'.

To take this old-school style to its highest expression demands going beyond mental recitation. The speaker must memorise the speech to the level of embodiment. This means knowing it to the point where you can recite the speech backwards, forwards, and starting at any point.

You should be able recite it in the same way you can drive without thinking about the pressure of the pedals or wheel in your hands.

Why? Because when you know it this well your attention is no longer consumed with thinking about what word comes next and you can now be present with your audience, to make eye contact and move naturally, which is what allows your essence to come through. Your essence is what people are touched by and fall in love with. It is the depth of your personality. It is life itself emerging through you in its own unique way. It is what we we all yearn for.

Unfortunately, with the old-school approach, most people never take it to that level of mastery. It takes an incredible amount of time and dedication. It could make sense if you were getting paid top dollar and repeating that same keynote for a whole year, but most people are not in that position. Therefore they end up on stage reciting instead of presenting and never allow for their essence to come through.

As social creatures we are always looking to create safety for ourselves. In this old-school method safety is created by controlling all the variables with the memorisation of every word and gestures so there are less variables in anything 'going wrong'. In the second model, this sense of safety we yearn for is created through genuine relationship with your audience.

So, enter, Method 2 ;)

Method #2: Embodied, Enlivened Speaking

This model was essentially my path into speaking and what I offer you here.

In this model, we flip the previous model backwards.

Instead of starting with a perfectly rehearsed speech, here we start with your essence. We start with what makes YOU come alive. This means allowing your essence to shine through you — it doesn't matter what you call it — authenticity, presence or magical pixie dust. The words don't matter as much as the feeling. It is when you are being most yourself, and showing people the real you. When we present from here, everything we do is magnetic and the audience will yearn for more of it.

The Enlivened Speaking Method

Essence / Authenticity / Presence
Here we begin with YOU and what makes you unique and it flows into all elements below.

Connection
Be genuine & relate to the audience authentically.

Content & Structure
Bullet-point all relevant information for the talk and arrange it for the audience and duration.

Speak & Influence
Because you are bringing your essence, you are naturally engaging and enlivening.

In the Enlivened speaking model we begin with utilising presence to ensure it filters down into everything else we do. Presence is what allows us to feel safe on stage and engage the audience without a script, create genuine rapport with them, and learn how to engage them with the content. The structure in this is not memorised but fluid. This allows us to hone our message and navigate how to land it in the most powerful and clear way with the audience.

The gold in starting with your essence is that you cannot help but be engaging. You are giving people all of you, and this depth of openness naturally creates connection. It is what we deeply yearn for as human beings — to feel connected, understood, and a sense of belonging.

There is quite an obvious creative tension that arises with this model though: vulnerability. We as people are habitually afraid of being truly seen and do everything we can to wear a social mask and avoid 'being real.' I had a new student say to me, "*Miroslav in this one session I feel I've connected more deeply with you than my closest friends. This is SO real!*" As the Enlivened approach demands beginning WITH the core of who we are, it will likely also bring up more emotion as we risk being judged by putting our real selves out there. Fears, insecurities etc. will naturally have the opportunity to arise and be integrated through the process. The Enlivened Method invites us into relationship with courage. We all have courage, yet some of us have never had the opportunity to genuinely practise it. Speaking is the opportunity.

The payoff in applying the Enlivened approach is massive though. Instead of all that time and commitment going into just memorising words for one presentation, you are creating authentic confidence and building a foundation with the deepest parts of who you are. This is a powerful way of being that will enhance all areas of your life regardless of whether you give another speech or not! For example one of my students Carolyn reflected how as she began studying at the institute she found herself speaking up more frequently at work meetings and even during team gatherings. Another student, Linda, who works in corporate found that as she worked on her own speaking with the institute she now had more confidence to stand up for other women in the workplace who didn't have a voice or couldn't speak up for themselves. THIS is the power of finding our authentic voice through the Enlivened method.

Engagement As The Norm

If we were to use a simple metaphor, the old-school method is like going out for coffee with a friend and memorising everything you will say, then speaking *at* them for an hour. (They probably won't invite you out again). In the Enlivened Method, you are receptive, listening and engaging with both their verbal and non-verbal cues. You both feel connected and alive during the conversation as you are having it together.

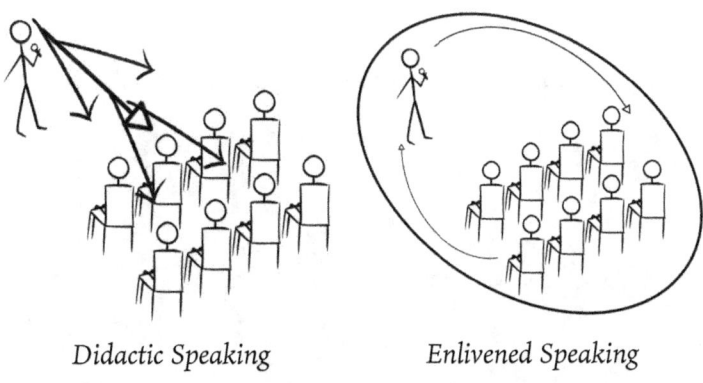

Didactic Speaking   *Enlivened Speaking*

Using the Enlivenment Method, engagement goes from being something you try and control using *'technique'* and *'hooks'* to just becoming *normal* — *the audience is engaged because you are being yourself.* It seems simple right? Yet we have created so many ways of controlling public speaking because we are afraid of being seen by anyone but our closest friends. But what if you were to bring more of the authentic person you are, in your home, family and intimate life to the stage?

With the Enlivened Speaking model you are *continually* in rapport with and engaging your audience because you are being seen and seeing them. Calling it engagement becomes arbitrary because the whole room is present and alive. The feeling is similar to the state when you are in a deep and meaningful conversation with a friend and both are just openly and easily listening.

Imagine standing on stage and recreating *that* with a room full of people.

You literally *magnetise* people into your world.

Enlivened Transmission: The Fast Way of Learning

Getting to the level where we can do this takes time. I had been practising meditation a few years before I began getting on stage in this way. After years of practising, I discovered that when I began to teach students in this way, what had taken me years to cultivate, they were learning in a fraction of the time. I have students in my 6 week training that find after only a couple of weeks they already have major breakthroughs and are more confident in front of others. One of my Russian students, Emma, explained that after just a few weeks into the program she had the confidence to do live videos in Russian. She had never done this before and her friends immediately recognised that she was more dynamic and confident! (They had no idea that she had been doing this course with me).

Typically at the end of our courses students are offered the opportunity to do a grad show and without fail they are amazed at how much they have learnt and internalised through the process without even knowing they had learnt it. This new way of speaking has just become a part of them in the time we had spent together, even though they did not do repetitive practice or memorisation.

When the students attention is completely with the teacher it seems to allow for more embodiment and information transfer. Some people call it learning through osmosis.

Students are able to build a relationship to the content being taught a lot quicker. It goes from being an idea to an embodied experience. On one hand this is perhaps why we have always been attracted to studying with masters in their respective fields. The Enlivened method has extracted the blueprint of why this works and developed it further.

The gift of learning in this way has a major advantage for teachers and students. Firstly, as teachers deliver through applying an embodied approach we are meeting any of the emotional resistance that is in the way of us being more authentic on stage. That means when we get up to present it is easier to be natural as we have already worked through the emotional resistance that is sabotaging us (fears, etc.). In rote or the old-school method which consists of repetition and memorisation this is not the case. We are basically memorising on top of the suppressed emotion we feel and in doing so disregarding the emotional and somatic (bodily) information that is present.

Secondly, and most importantly, we as students are fully engaged through-out the process in Enlivened speaking. Often what happens in education or presentation scenarios is what the great education scholar John Dewey (1933) would describe as that the pupil giving *"external, perfunctory attention to the teacher"* while the *"inmost thoughts are concerned with matters more attractive to [them]."*[7] The

---

7   Dewey, J. (1933). *How we think*. Buffalo, NY: Prometheus Books. (p. 33)

student may appear to be listening, but their awareness is not even in the room and their eyes are likely glazed over or in their phones. There is no learning without engagement. It is literally the bandwidth for information transfer. The more engagement/attention/presence there is in the room, the more data can be transmitted. When we teach through presence as the medium, the audience is genuinely engaged which in turn increases their learning and enjoyment of the experience. The audience's attention is fully able to receive what the speaker is offering. With the Enlivened approach we are marrying both the inner and outer worlds into the present moment, so the listeners are fully captivated.

The problem as noted before is that when we are using the old-school style we are 'prepared' but not *present*. One of my clients from Singapore, Jace Min articulated this well in her experience through training with me "*I spent a lot of my life trying to make my thinking and words powerful. I used to prepare more, and it used to use up a lot of my presence — which I knew I had but couldn't use. Now I have fun and feel at ease while presenting.*" Speaking is a natural expression, when we unravel our presence we allow all of us onto the stage which naturally invites the audience's presence to meet us.

Academic Research & The Magic of Presence

In 2020 I wrote an academic thesis researching on the effects of the Enlivened approach on yoga students I was teaching at the time. A part of this research included interviewing students about their experience when in class with me. This research and its findings will be cited a few times throughout this book as it supports the principles outlined. The principles you are about to read are not just theoretical ideas — but lived experience which has underpinned my speaking/teaching for close to a decade. This rigorous study was undertaken to unearth and understand what and how I was employing to create the success I had. The students I interviewed all cited experiences of being fully engaged, with some of their responses noted below:

"[I] wasn't thinking about anything else while you were teaching." — Nadia

"The whole time I'm on a journey in your class I just feel presence." — Fae

"Other teachers have that but it comes and goes, with you it's like we are there for the whole time and nothing is going to intrude." — Beatrice

Beatrice went on to detail the effects of my classes on her, referencing experiences with other teachers. When other teachers ask her to breathe, she said *"it goes over my head"* and she still finds herself not breathing while *"thinking of something outside of the room"* where as *"[Miroslav] certainly brings my mind into the room and nothing else seems to encroach into my thoughts."* This mirrors what John Dewey outlined earlier, as well as what many of us may have experienced at presentations, meetings and conferences. We are 'listening' externally, but our minds are elsewhere. As listeners this is likely because the speaker isn't fully present either.

With the Enlivened approach to the stage, we invite the audience into full presence — Internally and externally.

Goosebumps: The Science

The academic literature across science, medicine and education provides us with valuable information in understanding the tingling phenomenon. According to medicine tingling falls inside the general term paresthesia (sensations of a person's body with no apparent physical cause).[8] In the Education literature though goosebumps would be classed as *'affect.'* Dr. Mulcahy (2015) defines affective forces as *"intensities, sensations or energies that can be discharged through objects and spaces."*[9] Affect can be considered any force that affects the body and changes it in some way.[10]

Scientific papers examine and classify body tingling under a number of different factors. Some which are irrelevant for us (such as tingling induced by drugs, phantom limbs, etc.) and others which link tingling/chills/goosebumps to a variety of positive and negative emotions and arousal which can be grouped into the following two distinctions:

---

8   NINDS (2017). Paresthesia information page. National Institute of Neurological Disorders and Stroke. Retrieved August 7, 2017, from <https://www.ninds.nih.gov/Disorders/All-Disorders/Paresthesia-Information-Page>.

9   Mulcahy, D. (2015). Body matters: The critical contribution of affect in school classrooms and beyond. In B. Green & N. Hopwood (Eds.), *The body in professional practice, learning and education* (pp. 105-120). Cham, Switzerland: Springer International Publishing. (p. 108)

10 Borovica, T. (2017). Dancing the strata: Investigating affective flows of moving/ dancing bodies in the exploration of bodily (un)becoming. *Qualitative Inquiry, 25*(1), 26-36. doi: https://doi.org/10.1177/1077800417745919 2017

Cold Shivers — *linked to disgust, fear, sadness and avoidance motivation.*

Tingling-Goosebumps — *linked to greater surprise, enjoyment and approach motivation.*[11]

Tingling-goosebumps linked to positive outcomes are obviously the ones we want to elicit as speakers/teachers. Scientific papers link tingling to a number of affective states such as being energised and positive excitement.[12] Tihanyi and others (2017) conducted a literature analysis on large volumes of previously existing research on tingling. They synthesised only one model that explains every aspect of tingling they encountered. They named it *"The attention-disclosed model, i.e., attention discloses the sensation by opening the gate for suppressed sensory information."*[13]. In normal English this means that by bringing our attention to the body we are able perceive information which was already present but outside of our conscious awareness. For example it is like a time when your mind was busy with thoughts and after relaxing you begin to notice the atmospheric sounds around you which were always there

---

11 Maruskin, L. A., Thrash, T. M., & Elliot, A. J. (2012). The chills as a psychological construct: Content universe, factor structure, affective composition, elicitors, trait antecedents, and consequences. Journal of Personality and Social Psychology, 103(1), 135–157. http://dx.doi.org/10.1037/a0028117

12 Ayan, 2005; Bathmaker & Avis, 2005; Gould, 1991. *(See reference list)*.

13 Tihanyi, B. T., Ferentzi, E., Beissner, F., & Köteles, F. (2017). The neuropsychophysiology of tingling. Consciousness and Cognition, 58, 97–110. doi:10.1016/j.concog.2017.10.015

but outside of your conscious awareness. This is an example of suppressed sensory information becoming more available.

To extrapolate this further we could include both background information as above (atmospheric noise, body sensations, etc.) but also self-suppressed information such as thoughts and memories. This self-suppressed information is laying dormant in our nervous system at an intensity we can't recognise until it is revealed — perhaps by the words or intentions of another. In a speaking/teaching environment this could imply the person on stage directing our attention to what was suppressed and in doing so we know or recognise it on a deeper level. Thus goosebumps could be considered a tangible experience of the moment suppressed information becomes conscious. Another persons words can free up information that was seemingly invisible to us inside our own system. In essence, we could say goosebumps are indicators of connection: connection between each other and connection within ourselves.

The Goosebumps Formula

Outside of the scientific literature, goosebump experiences and their significance are worded differently by different people. One of my more logical friends describes goosebumps as *"the unconscious mind communicating to the conscious mind that this is important and needs to be paid attention to."* My Tantra teachers have referred to goosebumps as *"Shakti"* — or the movement of energy or consciousness in its most pure form.

Regardless of what definition we give it, the theme that continually appears is that these are powerful moments which capture our attention. Goosebumps make us notice what is happening and draw our attention to the present moment. They are moments which feel more 'real' than the repetitive cycles of life we often find ourselves in. It is as if they are a gentle nudge back out of a habitual numbness and into our aliveness.

Although there is no 'formula' to create goosebumps in a social context there is a common set of 'ingredients' that are typically present to evoke them. You can not force goosebumps upon someone (unless you want to terrify them, which is more the cold-chills type). In my understanding goosebumps are activated when we are in full alignment internally to what we are saying externally and this transmission has relevance for the listener. Our alignment is across all spheres: mentally, emotionally, philosophically and with the audience. When we are speaking our deepest truth, it touches other people in a somatic (bodily) way.

We can not feign 'goosebumps', they emerge from a place of surrendering to the depth of ourselves as you will discover through the principles in coming chapters. Instead of communicating what we know from the head, we are letting our essence, along with our ideas and emotions pour forth through us in the moment. The impulse for the words arises from our cells or presence and moves through us. It 'lands' as truth because the audience recognised it within themselves also. Not an absolute Truth, but genuine truth in that moment, which we recognise in the depth of our beings.

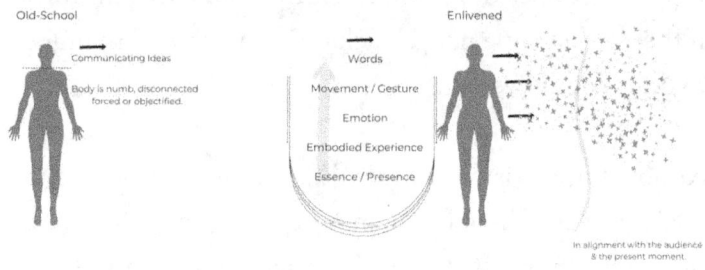

The two necessary ingredients that are almost always present are *alignment* and *connection*.

1. Alignment

Often there needs to be a great degree of personal presence from the person speaking. Whether this presence comes from the vulnerability of telling a new story, or from the capacity to hold the audience attention — without presence we can not have alignment. Additional to presence, the person speaking must also have a depth of embodiment or personal experience with their content — It is something they have experienced, lived and breathed. Thus when words emerge from this deeper place they are full of authenticity and genuine emotion. This is not faking or enacting emotion to create an effect as the audience's subconscious minds have a great capacity to detect misalignment. A study conducted by Stanford University found that when test subjects suppressed their emotions during conversation it not only disrupted communication, reduced rapport and inhibited the formation of relationship but also raised the subjects blood pressure as well as their listening partners.[14] You could say the stress was contagious. As speakers this means if we suppress our emotions/are not genuine and authentic we are affecting the rapport and stress of the audience also. On the other hand when the words emerge through us from emotional congruency they are imbued with a natural texturing which is genuine to the moment. We call this ***alignment.***

---

14   Butler, E. et al. (2003). The Social Consequences of Expressive Suppression. American Psychological Association, Inc. Emotion, Vol. 3, No. 1, 48–67 doi:10.1037/1528-3542.3.1.48

2. Connection

Connection is vital as goosebumps obviously always happen in relationship to someone or something. A great story which gives one audience goosebumps can fall flat on another audience. It is not 'content specific.' To be in the industry of goosebumps is the recognition that you are not a content machine but a living being, and need to be connected to whom you are speaking to. It's like someone telling a joke and getting lots of laughs one night, then trying the same joke with another group of friends and it doesn't land. They were attached to the content instead of recognising the relational field and context in which the words were spoken. Connection requires an awareness and responsiveness of whom we are speaking to and how to best communicate to them. Genuine connection also means opening up and really being seen by the audience instead of hiding behind social masks, insecurities, or 'performer' archetypes.[15]

So how do we create more alignment and connection? Well I'm glad you asked as the next four chapters are dedicated to explaining just this.

---

[15] Note: Performance can be genuine and when it is we probably call it art, in the context used here the performer archetype is the disconnected version where we 'perform' so we are not really seen.

A Little Bonus

In my six month Mastery trainings we go deep into the hidden world behind speaking. One of the levels we explore is how we imbue our words with the 'felt sense' we speak them from. For example saying I love you when you're angry is very different than saying it when you actually feel the love for someone. The words are just the carriers of the emotion or felt sense from which they arise. Sometimes the simplest of words communicated from the right place is far more powerful than all the right words from the wrong place. (Ever felt someone apologise perfectly and feel nothing in response?... and at other times just a one word 'Sorry' can make you feel the depth of their acknowledgement). Enlivened speaking is about transmitting this level of communication.

This is very synonymous with the relationship to mantras within traditional Yogic paths. You may have heard of Mantra chanting, these are typically syllables or short phrases that are repeated to elicit a certain state. When you delve deeper into the teachings though you discover that they say a mantra is ineffective unless it is *'alive.'* A mantra imbued with life can come from one of two ways: Receiving it from a teacher who already has an established relationship with the Mantra, so that when they give it to you they are also transferring this relationship. Or the second way is to commit the time to create a relationship with the mantra yourself. The essence of this is mirrored not just in mantra but in all words. They carry the essence of the wisdom (or felt sense) from which they are spoken. The same words from two different people can go unnoticed or touch the depths of the heart.

4. Principle 1A: Cultivating Stage Presence

What Is The Stage?

Read this a couple of times,

What is the stage?

...

What, *is* the stage?

...

What is the *stage*?

Let these words marinate. What is it? What is its purpose?

What does it mean to you? Let's Consider this for a few moments before we go on. It is very important as this relationship is crucial to everything you do from here on.

So, let's flesh this out.

Last year, as a new student, Maria, was enrolling into my online speaking program she said,

"But Miroslav, how will we do speaking without a stage?"

I laughed, "*Maria, the stage is in your head. If I asked you to stand and present now as if you are on stage, all the same fears would come up as if you were actually on stage.*"

I have had people book sessions in with me and convince me they are completely fine with public speaking until I ask them to stand up and present: then they go blank and try to back-peddle with small talk. One woman was like "*Oh my god I am so nervous right now.*" Yes, yes, you are. But why?

The Stage Is Your Power

The stage is not just a platform to stand on.

The stage is a relationship to our own power. It will show you where in your life you are running from your power. It will teach you to let go of the old parts of you where you were playing small, and invite you to jump off the cliff and discover what is possible on the way down.

It is not for everyone.

You will not be the same person on the other side.

Every time you get on a stage in an Enlivened way you will evolve.

How?...

The Unseen Truth

The stage is essentially *any* relational or power dynamic where there are many people listening to one person.

This includes speaking, teaching, facilitating, work meetings, yoga teaching, singing, stand-up comedy, dancing, stand-up poetry, graduation dinners, auctions, toasts, etc.

Equally so any digital platform such as zoom conferences, meetings, Facebook lives, etc.

The above are all different variations of *'the stage.'*

The stage is an educative outlet where information is exchanged — in everything from keynote presentations to work meetings. It is a place where teaching and learning happens (whether obviously or not) and new relationships are created. Thus, you will find throughout this book I have quoted some of the most important research conducted within the fields of education and teaching as this application of 'the stage' is far more studied than just public speaking. There is far more research about students and teachers than speakers and listeners even though they are fundamentally a very similar relationship.

The relational dynamic of 'one speaking to many' that stages create turn them into places of power. In our day-to-day social situations power is distributed in calculated ways. It moves through our habitual identities which are formed through this relationship to power. As an example there is generally always the loud person that wants all the attention, whether it is your uncle at the barbecue or the obnoxious guy at work. Then other people fall around this person. This mix of dominant and submissive personalities automatically find their place within social settings. This means our behaviours and expressions generally fall into the repetitive patterns we are accustomed to and most comfortable with. Additionally we reinforce this by continually telling ourselves consciously and unconsciously that '*this is who we are*' because it is the role we play most often in life. The stage lets us flip this whole dynamic. The old rules no longer apply, and you don't have to pretend to be your 'social self.'

This is why Steve Martin said "*sometimes introverts make the best comedians*"[16], because they get on stage to express everything they haven't been able to in everyday life. I would agree with him. On a stage power is focused on one person as they are being listened to by many. By focusing and summoning peoples' attention to one person EVERYTHING is amplified. This has advantages and challenges. The challenges are obvious, for most people it is just too much to handle. Their system gets overloaded with the attention and they get nervous, pace, stutter or go completely blank.

Sometimes new speakers try to soldier through the

---

16   Masterclass. (Publication date not offered). *Steve Martin Teaches Comedy* [Video]. Masterclass. https://www.masterclass.com/classes/steve-martin-teaches-comedy

challenges and suppress the emotion by reciting their script but the body does not lie. The nervousness will come out sideways through the tone of their voice, nervous jitters, awkward hand gestures or filler words (*um, ah, eh, like*, etc.). If you have ever seen someone on stage do this, you may have turned to the person next to you and said, "I have no idea what they just said, all I got from that is how nervous they were."

As a metaphor you could imagine every audience member like the charge inside a battery. As they are all seated together that is a lot of potential energy. When all of this energy is focused on the speaker, they will likely go into contraction because far more of them is being seen than they are used to. It will push to the surface anything that has been stuck within that person's life (nerves, fears, insecurities, etc.).

When a person is on stage they are broadcasting information *all* the time, and every single nuance in their voice and physical movement is being MAGNIFIED by the amount of attention the audience is placing on them. Therefore whether we are aware of it or not, we are constantly communicating on *so* many levels.

The stage *is* a magnifying glass for what has been stuck inside us. Although the challenge is obvious, the virtue is even greater! The stage will bring to the surface parts of ourselves we have been hiding from in other areas of our life also: relationships, sexuality, finances, social, etc. The fear, resistance, nervousness, worries and anxiety that shows up on the stage has been buried in our systems for years and the stage has the power to draw it out of us. As I've mentioned before it is normal for me to receive messages from students after they have worked with me telling me how this training has influenced other areas of their life. They have said things like:

"Miroslav, even the conversations I have off the stage are so much better now!"

"I got a much higher paying job. I never would have had the confidence to do before this training!"

"I am so much more confident now!"

"I can now see my message and my purpose!"

"I am having so much more fun when I am on stage now."

"I am so much more confident even in social conversations"

And one of my favourites...

"It has even improved my sexuality! My head jobs are better now!"

(Haha, yes that was a real message!).

The above is not typical of all stage work. Most speaker trainings will teach you how to write, rehearse and recite speeches. The above are a result of of practising the Enlivened Method because we are utilising the stage as a tool to create deeper connection and embodiment with our personal and stage presence.

Magnification of Words

Remember how we said the stage is a magnifying glass? Well, imagine what happens when the fear and nerves are out of the way. What is being magnified now?

Your message.

All that attention being focused on you will add even more power to your words, actions and intentions. Your very presence will begin to emanate through the room without you needing to raise your voice. If you want a good example of this watch Dr. Martin Luther King Jr. *I Have A Dream* introduction. There is no loss of focus. Every moment of silence is poised with potential. We hang on his every word. No-one needs to be asked to listen when he brings so much presence to the stage.

Ever wonder why so many musicians get addicted to the stage? Watch Stevie Wonder or Freddie Mercury when they are fully present with the audience in live environments. It is electric! I remember seeing Stevie Wonder live in concert in Melbourne back in 2008. Every time he smiled it felt like he sparked off sunshine inside us and we would all smile with him. The whole arena lit up. The experience of speaking from this place of connection and aliveness is intoxicating. The 'stage-high' is a real thing. It is not about being an amazing performer though, but simply allowing yourself to meet the presence of the room without shrinking from it.

It is common for first time students in my trainings to report feeling elated, high or blissful for a day or two after being on stage for the first time. Some of them compared the highs to experiences they had previously only experienced on drugs. These experiences fundamentally lift the ceiling on what we believe is possible in our life. They touch our deepest parts. There was clinical studies conducted on subjects consuming magic mushrooms for the first time. Two years after the research 58% of subjects rated their mushroom experience as *"being among the five most personally meaningful"* and 62% rated it as among the *"five most spiritually significant experiences of their lives"*[17], next to getting married and their first child.

What my students and I have both discovered is that the stage is quite similar. It is a threshold that opens us to who we really are and changes our lives forever.

And... it does more.

---

17   Griffiths, R., Richards, W., Johnson, M., McCann, U., & Jesse, R. (2008). abstract

Choosing Presence Over Avoidance

Building this relationship with life and the stage is something that happens as a result of how we live. Generally most people stick to small talk and go through life fearing judgement. They reserve opening themselves only to those closest to them. Even then it usually takes a couple of drinks or sitting around the campfire. In my teens I used to drink a lot so I could let my walls down enough to have any kind of genuine experience of connection with people. I was naturally pent-up, defensive and avoidant of intimacy. Although it was necessary for me at the time, I recognised I was wanting more from life and would never be happy continuing like this. I gave up using alcohol as a social crutch and decided to face the fire and feel the discomfort I had been avoiding with alcohol. Facing the fire draws us more fully into our presence as we are choosing to no longer run from life but to face it head-on. It meant choosing to feel my insecurities, and speak my truth anyway.

When we can tap into this presence on stage, we allow the stage to become a reservoir for life itself. We know that every time we get on a stage it will connect us to life, to presence, and through this we can connect the audience to it too. *It is literally watching magic happen.* This process can be cultivated by understanding and utilising Meta-fear which we will unpack in the next chapter.

5.
Principle 1B: Meta-Fear, Vulnerability, Courage & Goosebumps

Often we think we have to avoid or overcome fear to own a stage, but in fact it is the complete opposite. Owning our fear and going through it is where the magic is. Brene Brown tells the story of how when preparing for her Tedx talk she realised it would not suffice just to talk about the vulnerability research she had conducted. It became evident to her that she would have to let *herself be vulnerable* on stage. When she first told her husband of her plans he asked her not to do it, but she knew it was what she had to do and persevered. Despite a massive vulnerability hangover that followed days to come, her talk is now in the top five most watched Ted talks ever. The success speaks for itself and her story highlights a major principle in the Enlivened approach: It is through our vulnerability and embracing our fear that we harness our potential.

Meta-Fear: Using Fear as a Tool for Presence

Working with enlivenment we will undoubtedly come across fear. Fear is probably the biggest obstacle to people employing the Enlivened approach in the first place as we seem to think that with enough 'planning' fear won't come up. But fear doesn't work like that. In fact we want it to come up, but what we want to do is change our relationship to it. These silly assertions that we need to suppress or 'smash our fears' all arise from an improper understanding and relationship to fear.

In her book *Scream*, Margee Kerr writes about studies on fear which were conducted on Tibetan monks who had an established meditation practise. What the researchers discovered is that the presence obtained through meditation allowed the monks to bring more attention to the somatic (bodily) experience, and then consciously decide what to make the sensations mean:

"Our sympathetic nervous system becomes aroused and then we interpret the arousal with cognitive manipulation and coordination between the limbic system and prefrontal cortex."[18]

In plain English this means they were able to separate the sensations in their body (fear, constriction, etc.) from the

---

18 Kerr, M. (2017). Scream: Chilling Adventures In The Science of Fear. Public Affairs.

stories that their mind was creating about the fear, giving them the capacity to interpret it in different ways. Basically the physical experience of fear has **no** inherent meaning except for the one our mind unconsciously creates and links to it. This 'meaning making' is happening all the time, the mind is on auto-pilot constantly turning sensations into meanings. Typically though we are often not aware it is happening, unless like the monks we have the awareness to separate the physical sensations from their mental counterparts.

For example imagine you see someone you are attracted to and your mind begins to race:

"Will they like me? What will they think of me? Should I ask them out? What should I say?"

The fear in your body is running the show and your mind is now trying to work out what to do on the surface layer. Unfortunately you are not even aware of where in your body the fear/sensations are showing up. What the previously mentioned research shows us is that when we can separate and integrate the fear we can choose what to make it mean on a cognitive or surface level.

Fear In Different Cultures

For some cultures and traditions the relationship to fear is fundamentally different. Before we dive into it, this chapter will use the 'G' word. Consider that 'God' in this context is not the bearded guy in the sky. What we may translate as 'God' in English through the lens of some yogic schools (Tantra, Advaita Vedanta) is actually closer to the experience of non-duality. Non-duality can be defined as the experience of being in direct relationship to everything in life. You may have spontaneously felt this in times of great awe or relaxation; when the mind is completely clear and you feel an inner peace inside and more connected to other people, nature etc. Non-duality is a feeling of oneness with all of life and the experience of this as our regular operating system.

A true spiritual path is one of seeking out to be in this relationship regardless of what is happening in life. Whether it is fear, anger, grief, or joy, we meet life through the spaciousness of non-duality. Instead of objectively thinking about life, we meet it with the body, with the sensations, with its aliveness. This allows the possibility to continually be in relation to life itself.

Now imagine what it would mean to meet fear in this context? If fear had no inherent meaning or story but was simply an influx of sensations. Imagine it as if you were the ocean, and fear was simply a wave moving through you. What kind of freedom does that offer?

Sally Kempton, a traditional Tantra teacher offers the following quote, a paraphrasing from a Tantrik Text:

> *"God who frees us from fear appears*
> *to the unenlightened as fear itself"*[19]
> **— Sally Kempton**

Let's take this apart for a moment and look closer at the words and their meaning. *Unenlightened* is referring to those with improper awareness or understanding. Enlightenment is not speaking about some accomplished state, but relational to fear. There is a clear distinction between how the enlightened (or those with awareness) experience fear, compared to those that are not abiding in awareness. According to this line, people that can abide in awareness and recognition of this text will *recognise fear AS God* (ie. recognising fear as a doorway to our full potential moves us deeper into relationship with that full potential, with life). For those without the awareness or understanding, they mistakenly misinterpret the experience as fear and steer away from it.

In the Jewish tradition Rabbi Alan Lew outlines two different Hebrew words commonly translated as fear. One is *pachad*, which is akin to the type of experiences one would prefer to avoid, and the second is *yirah (Norah)*. *Yirah*, although commonly translated to fear, is closer to the

---

19   Kempton, S. (2014) Doorways To The Infinite: The Art & Practise of Tantric Meditation. Sounds True. (Audible Timestamp: *Chapter: Bhairava, The Inner Guru 3:44*).

English word *awe*.[20] In the Bible it was used to describe the experience of meeting God (again this word). Rabbi Lew describes *yirah* as being overwhelmed by the amount of energy or sensation running through our body. As above, if we are not accustomed or do not have understanding, we panic. Alternatively if we lean into it, we can let this experience open us to life.

---

20 Lew, A. (2005). *Be Still And Get Going: A Jewish Meditation Practise For Real Life*. Little Brown & Company. (p. 48).
(*Note: Lew uses 'norah' in his writings which is the adjectival form. Yirah is the noun form of the same word*).

Separating Story From Sensation

The relationship we have to fear fundamentally changes when met through presence as it becomes a part of our embodied experience. From presence we are able to remain in awareness as the fear rises, but it is not labelled as fear — just experienced as energy and sensation. It can move through us and we can remain in the eye of the storm so to speak. Instead of running from it as we did in the past, we recognise it for what it is and turn towards it. We breathe in and welcome the experience to move through us. Fear met in this way engages us and brings us more fully into life. It becomes a beautiful lovemaking experience where as we lean into it, it becomes even more pleasurable.

The key difference is that there are no stories attached to the sensations in the body, we are not making it mean anything. At first it takes practice to do this, but after a while you just begin to relate to it differently. I teach this process in more depth in my Meta-Fear short course where we unpack and embody this more powerful relationship to fear and courage.[21]

The excitement that arises with fear is the recognition that we do not know what will happen or who we will be on the other side of the experience that fear is inviting us into. For someone that has never been on stage there is no reference point for what will happen on or after the stage. Will they

---

21 More information on Meta-fear and other courses offered by ESI can be found at the back of this book.

be laughed at or shunned? The mind lives based on patterns and experiences of the past. When we begin to utilise fear through the Enlivened Method it becomes a doorway to experiencing the fullness of who we can become. By not knowing what will happen we embrace the unknown, we embrace possibility. To use another metaphor you could say we are writing a new algorithm that has not existed within us before.

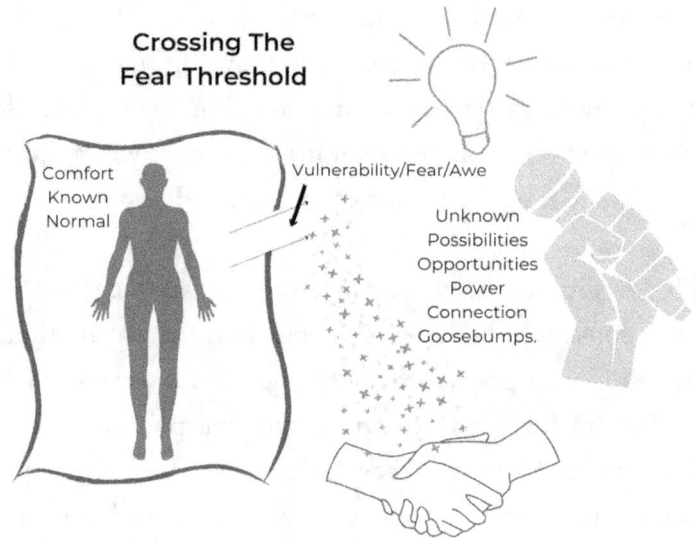

Fear is the gateway into our full potential. We could loosely refer to this potential as God, but in reality it is our full unrealised self. The self we were born to be when we let go of control and do not know what will happen next. The self that is here when we are in the deepest relationship with life. It is the experience of being and moving with life as opposed to controlling and striving through the safety and predictability of the mind. It is more risky and more fun, because it is CLOSER to life.

Metaphorically it is like going from practising riding a surfboard on the sand, to taking it out into the ocean where you do not have control of the ocean but have to be in relationship to it. The unpredictability and invitation to respond in real time is what makes it exciting. It is why people get addicted to extreme sports — but we do not have to put our lives on the line to experience this rush, freedom, and connection to reality.

We simply have to open our hearts and let life meet us. It means walking with more authenticity and courage, and speaking about the things we have been holding back. Life, from here, becomes full, magnificent and unknown. All these words serve only to connect us to *that*. When we are in relationship to *it, it becomes louder than any words in any language*. Life draws us forwards.

Now you may think you find this experience once and that's it, it's there forever. But no. We must continue reconnecting to this current, to life, over and over again. For it is not a destination but a relationship. And public speaking is the most direct link I have found into living life in this way. The beauty of this is; all you need is your presence and to get on stage. Unlike sports or other methods where your body and age may be obstacles, anyone can get on stage and communicate. The more fear there might be, the more powerful it becomes when you express yourself.

This experience of what happens when presence and fear are utilised in this way is perhaps best paraphrased by one of my students parents who watched her and the others speak at the Graduation Show for one of my programs. Stacey Molengraaf who's dad was a preacher said to her after afterwards,

"I finally understand what you meant when you said embodiment. Your whole bodies were there! If you were at the front of the church, God would have just soared out of your fricken' body because you were just there!"

This is the power of presence. And this is the power of Enlivened, embodied speaking. Taking the level of presence of awe that people typically experience in mystical or religious settings, and channelling it into all the important topics we are here to speak about.

Vulnerability Is Not What You Think It Is

Vulnerability is frequently confused and misunderstood. People sometimes mistake vulnerability as a weak person in the fetal position. Sure, this can be one example of it. More correctly though vulnerability means to act with courage, to keep listening and moving with our life calling, our purpose, and expressing what genuinely arises from this. It is vulnerable because we do not know what will happen if we follow life in this way. It is continually saying *yes to life* as opposed to the comfort of our pre-existing patterns. To echo the words of researcher Brene Brown:

> "Courage is a heart word. The root of the word courage is cor — the Latin word for heart. In one of its earliest forms, the word courage meant "To speak one's mind by telling all one's heart."[22]

Professor M. Bache writes in his book *The Living Classroom* that the energy of the classroom is the strongest when we as the teachers meet students at our edge.[23] To explore our edge is vulnerable yet it also invites us into presence. What I have discovered having coached hundreds of people on speaking is the following: Vulnerability can show up in a variety of forms and is different for every person. It can

---

[22] TED. (2011, Jan 4). *The power of vulnerability | Brené Brown* [Video]. Youtube. https://youtu.be/iCvmsMzlF7o

[23] Bache, C. M. (2008). The Living Classroom: Teaching And Collective Consciousness. SUNY Press.

be the raising of one's voice, telling a story, getting angry, slowing down, or even smiling. Sometimes, just breathing on stage in silence will make people feel vulnerable (hence why so many people talk fast on stage to avoid actually feeling what's going on in their body).

The key thing here is that whenever we test or extend our identity we face vulnerability. In this case consider your identity, the person you are most often: the pace you speak, mannerisms you use, eye contact you make etc. We tend to avoid expressions that are not within our norm. When we have to do something that is not within our usual sphere of expression — we have to move through vulnerability to get there. It feels new, and we are likely being seen in it for the first time, or the first time by new people. If it is a small extension in our personality we can usually just slide into it, where as if it is a lot more vulnerable than what we're used to we may say something like *'well that's just not me'* and avoid extending ourselves into this new expression. I know this because I have said it so many times myself. Yes, at first, it wasn't me. And after life came through me in that way, it has become another aspect or expression of me, just as it will for you.

The patterns that we hold in our behaviours are often unconsciously ingrained. There was seminal research conducted in the 1980's that studied the length of time teachers would pause after asking a question. It was less than one second! This exposes two very important tenets.

The first as the author explained, was that these brief pauses do not allow *"an adequate exchange of ideas and the nurturing of new ideas cannot take place."*[24] Secondly, to me this work highlights our levels of discomfort and vulnerability with silence, with being exposed or unsure about what will happen next. Minimising the unknown creates an experience of control, but in fact it is fuelled by an underlying fear.

We cannot compare vulnerabilities between people.

What is vulnerable for one person may be normal for another.

Everyone's life, experiences, and nervous systems are different.

All that matters is that you are leaning into your own vulnerabilities and aliveness.

This is where growth happens.

In the old-school speaking model students are generally taught to find a vulnerable story from their lives which they can then keep retelling every time they speak. Usually this is a story of how they came from hard beginnings, heart break, etc. The first few times they tell it the story will

---

24   Rowe, M. B. (1986). Wait Time: Slowing Down May Be A Way of Speeding Up! *Journal of Teacher Education, 37*(1), 43–50. doi: 10.1177/002248718603700110 (p. 48)

likely be vulnerable as they are exposing parts of themselves which are dear to their hearts. But as it is repeated the story becomes a normal part of their expression and if they try and force the vulnerability it looks fake. It has lost its aliveness. This is what I call 'acting vulnerable'.

There is a *big* difference between acting vulnerable and feeling vulnerable. When we are experiencing vulnerability we are transmitting aliveness. THIS is what gives people goosebumps! If you remember the definition from the previous chapter in regards to goosebumps being our nervous system opening and acknowledging new information is emerging. What we as speakers are leaning into is evoking this. Vulnerability as a feeling, emerges when we are genuinely stepping through the threshold of an established pattern of behaviour we know well and decide to express ourselves in a new way we have not done before.

Through this model vulnerability is not the goal; it is a signpost or threshold that we are meeting an edge. As you lean into aliveness, vulnerability will show up.

The free workbook which is an accompaniment to this book is available at **www.enlivenedspeaking.com/bonus** and will provide you with simple tools to connect more powerfully with your authentic vulnerability.

6.
Principle 2: Power of Relationship

Early on, I discovered that presence was not just a phenomenon happening inside me but that it emerges through relationship with others. If we are around someone who is abiding in deeper presence than our current state, our nervous system calms down and we naturally come into presence ourselves (and vice-versa). As speakers, when we connect and build rapport with a room of people we can go deeper into presence together. When I first began teaching I found that if I could bring my students into presence, their presence would gravitate me more deeply into presence also. We are communal creatures. Hufford (2014) writes of presence as a mutual experience created between teachers and students describing it as *"an intellectual/emotional connecting of teacher and students—that allows a classroom of individuals to become an inclusive learning community."*[25]

---

25   Hufford, D. (2014). Presence in the classroom. *New Directions for*

This became most evident to me many years ago when I went to a healing centre to listen to another speaker. This was before I had actively begun speaking. At one point of his talk he asked for questions and my heart began pounding (Meta-fear) and I knew I had to ask. I raised my hand reluctantly, already feeling my heart beat racing. I was sitting at the back and as he invited my question all the eyes in the room turned to face me. The fear began to flood through me. I could literally hear my heartbeat in my head. My mind went quiet. I took a few deep breaths, closed my eyes and settled into myself and the intensity of sensation. I then felt the question and asked. I don't remember what I asked but I recall the woman next to me exclaiming with wide eyes,

"Did you see what you just did to the room?!" I noticed everyone in the room was mirroring her wonder while peering at me.

"No..." I replied confused.

"You just brought us all into stillness!" Wow. I reflected to myself. Here I was again thinking to myself that an experience was just happening inside me, when in fact what happens inside us when the attention is on us, affects everyone around us.

Education research heavily backs the value of relationship in teaching and learning. In 2017 a major report on Australian education utilising evidence-based recommendations

---

Teaching and Learning, 2014(140), 11-21. doi: 10.1002/tl.20109 (p. 14)

to improve engagement and learning in classroom environments advocated for strong relationships as one of its main suggestions.[26] This relational nature of teaching and learning is frequently reported in the literature on both embodiment (see for example[27]) and authenticity (see for example[28]). It is through relationship that trust, respect and safety are created. In the research I conducted through interviews with my own students they consistently referenced the relational nature of the Enlivened Method and how it affected them:

"You like us all to connect as a group. Which makes me feel quite safe." — Beatrice

"Sometimes you become the collective, sometimes you are at the front and you are sharing and showing and sometimes you are at the back." — Fae

"I feel happier, we got more talking, connection." — Katie

"There is positive energy around me so I probably benefit from them a lot more than I realise." — Nadia

By having my awareness *on* the relationship with

---

26 Goss, P., Sonnemann, J., & Griffiths, K. (2017). *Engaging students: creating classrooms that improve learning* (No. 2017-01). Retrieved from https://grattan.edu.au/wp-content/uploads/2017/02/Engaging-students-creating-classrooms-that-improve-learning.pdf (p. 21)

27 Forgasz 2019; Latta & Buck, 2008; Munro 2018.

28 Brook 2009; Cranton & Carusetta, 2004; Kreber, 2007; Rodgers & Raider-Roth 2006.

participants instead of an internal plan or dialogue, students in my research reported feeling more "safe" (Beatrice). This meant they were engaged and willing to open up, to be present. Students additionally went on to explain how this depth of relationship they had in sessions with me rippled into other areas of their life as the presence affected their intimate, social and work lives.

Speaking & Life Is All About Relationship

Enlivened Speaking is so magnetic because it positions the speaker and audience at the epicentre of what it means to be human: relationship. As mentioned in the old-school model we cultivate a sense of safety and stability through memorisation, repetition and recitation which cuts us off from life. In the Enlivened Speaking Model we create stability through the relationship we create with ourselves and our audience. As Parker Palmer, the great education writer, argued, *"Technique is what teachers use until the real teacher arrives."* This bears similarity to an enlivened approach. Palmer (1998) urged teachers to focus on *"who is the self that teaches?"*[29] which is also at the centre of the Enlivened method.

EVERYTHING in the human life is based on relationship and relating. This was a major *aha!* moment for me when I discovered relationships were not just between people, but also between people and everything else in their lives. Consider for example your relationship to sports, money, sex, or nature. Your friends probably have different relationships to all of these things. The things themselves do not change, only our relationship to them does. As we learn to relate to these elements in different ways, life opens up to us.

---

29 Palmer, P. J. (1998). *The courage to teach: exploring the inner landscape of a teacher's life*. San Francisco, CA: Jossey-Bass. (p.7)

Consider perhaps when you first started a new sport, hobby or business. At first, everything was new and you learnt the basics, but as your relationship with the discipline developed you began to see finer distinctions which were invisible to you at first. Mastery of any skill is essentially the degree of distinctions that we can embody. For example when I first began mountain biking I was unconsciously bracing my whole body throughout the first ride which left me unnecessarily sore. As I rode more I began to recognise the nuances of letting my body weight become fluid and using it to corner easier and feel the terrain under my tyres. This was achieved through time spent on the trails, and coaching from people that knew more than me. Time and coaching allowed me to develop and deepen my relationship with mountain biking. I have seen people who know all the strategies but still their business is failing. Why? Because of their relationship to it. You could break this down into not having enough drive, direction or whatever but I would begin fundamentally by exploring their relationship to business first. If the relationship is off, for example the person is unconsciously relating to business as hard work or a chore, they will likely avoid doing what needs to be done.

Who we are and how we live is determined by our relationships. Our relationship to business, to nature, to exercise — the objects themselves have no inherent meaning, it is in how we relate to them that we create the meaning which then informs our actions towards it.

The Golden Triangle:
3 Key Relationships of Speaking

The Golden Triangle is a teaching device I created to explain the three most important and dynamic relationships for the speaker/teacher. Without these, the best content in the world would fall flat.

The Golden Triangle

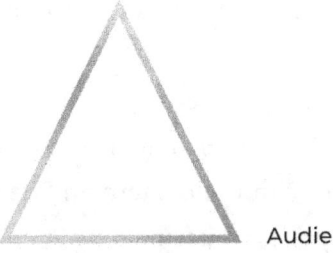

Content
This is expertise, message, what it is you are speaking about.

Speaker
This is you. Your role is to build a relationship to the audience, then support them to build a relationship to your content.

Audience
The audience is always changing. Even the same audience will feel and think differently if you speak to them twice.

Speaker and Audience — This is the primary relationship. It is what creates trust, rapport, engagement and likability. If you genuinely connect with your audience they will like and listen to you. Even if they do not agree, the sheer fact that you are showing up and being present will ensure they give you their attention. If you get this right, you will stand out compared to most other speakers out there.

Speaker and Content — This is your relationship to your own content. Ideally if you are speaking in your own expertise you can recite this in your sleep without problem. It is what you love, what you study and what you always speak about. Your content is likely what is the highest on your list of values, and the deeper your relationship with your content, the less you need to rehearse it as it already lives inside you. If you are speaking about topics which are not the ones you have studied most, it will likely take more time to research and plan. You would have to draw on your life experiences and existing research to find how the pieces link together and what you want to present.

Audience and Content — This is where you connect your content to your audience so they can refine their relationship with the content and develop deeper insight from what you are offering. It is the purpose and magic of your talk. You are the medium that allows your audience to create a relationship with the content you have expertise in. You essentially put yourself on the line to become the bridge for your listeners to build their own relationship to the topics you have mastery in.

A Secret Tip: Enticing Content

Parker Palmer (1998), who was mentioned earlier, taught that to create an engaging teaching style it is necessary to incorporate the relating *"big stories"* (the disciplines or subject matter) to *"small stories"* (personal experience) so students may establish a personal relationship with the content.[30] For example when I first watched Guy Ritchies King Arthur the big story was obviously the action packed myth. The small story though was how this myth began to affect my relationship with life. It allowed me to see that both the bad and good characters in the film were just aspects of me. The 'bad guy' inside me was what was pushing and pressuring the courageous part of me (the good guy) to come forth and succeed. I began to see the patterns from the film in my own life. If studying history, the big story is what happened, the small story is how it affects us as people today etc. If we as speakers spend too much time in the small stories it becomes meaningless as it is just personal experience. Focusing too much in big stories provides lots of data but risks being meaningless as it has no relationship to our everyday life.

It is through the merging of big and small stories that magic happens and makes the content relatable and engaging. I often see speakers and teachers miss this completely and get stuck in just communicating ideas or theory which

---

30   Palmer, P. J. (1998). *The courage to teach: exploring the inner landscape of a teacher's life*. San Francisco, CA: Jossey-Bass. (p.76)

quickly bores audiences. This disconnection from everyday life is emotionally a much safer place to be as a presenter. Through weaving a personal story into their presentation it often opens the gates of vulnerability and brings these ideas to life.

Entering The Shared Field

The three relationships described in The Golden Triangle are not just ideas, but living organisms. They become tangible experiences when we begin to present in this way. Lauren Becker was one of my clients who beautifully articulated the difference of speaking with a relational based approach instead of just presenting. At her first gig after completing my 6 month program she said; *"Oh my God Miroslav!... When I asked the audience a question I could FEEL their response rise in the room just as you said!"* When we are in presence and relationship with our audience — their responses to our questions arise in the room as if we were in one body of water. This is because our presence is with them and not with the pre-written script inside our head.

The audience is usually so deeply in the experience they have no awareness of the mechanics behind it. To get a sense of how this is experienced by listeners I asked Fae, one of my students. Speaking about the experience she said, *"My experience of you Miroslav, You're actually able to dissect yourself, to become the student, become the teacher, become the space."* She is speaking here to the experience of being in a shared field of consciousness. Professor Christopher Bache also wrote thoroughly of his and students' experiences with the shared group field and he explained the miss of most academics still believing that teaching happens purely as a transfer of information between two seperate minds that do not touch. He writes of how often he experienced this unified field operating below the surface of the mind and at times *"When the magic happened, the walls of our seperate minds seemed to come down temporarily"*[31]

This is reminiscent of researchers Dixon and Senior's (2011) similar description that *"the bodies of 'teachers' merge with/ extend to 'student' bodies"* through which *"a pedagogical unification is real and present."*[32] In simple terms this can be translated as a shared experience where the group experiences itself as one organism. It is akin to being in flow state and deeply immersed in the teaching/speaking experience. This can only happen through the presenter opening themselves up to create this depth of connection and it creates complete and total engagement.

If this idea is challenging or not one you have experienced, consider this: the body is a subjective experience that does not stop where our skin does. Our mind, emotions, and relationships are all embodied experiences which are continually interweaving with our environments. We do not exist in a vacuum — if you put the human body in outer space it dies. We are embedded in our environments. Consider therefore a deep and meaningful conversation or receiving a massage — we both naturally open up and occupy more space. When we are in an argument or stressed

---

31 Bache, C. M. (2008). The Living Classroom: Teaching And Collective Consciousness. SUNY Press. (p 22)

32 Dixon, M., & Senior, K. (2011). Appearing pedagogy: From embodied learning and teaching to embodied pedagogy. *Pedagogy, Culture & Society, 19*(3), 473-484. doi: 10.1080/14681366.2011.632514 (p. 473).

we experience contraction. The body exists as a part of its environment and thus is continually in relationship to it. The experiential nature of reality was first coined by French philosopher Merleau-Ponty as the phenomenological perspective. Instead of thinking of the mind and body as two separate entities as was popularised by Descartes and is still the dominant worldview today, Merleau-Ponty asserted that we are bodily by nature and thus inseparable from the body, hence everything bodily, all phenomena, are an inseparable part of the human experience.[33] When experiencing the world through the experiential body we perhaps enter Stolz's (2015) assertion that to *"Merleau-Ponty it is impossible to separate the unity of the mind and the body from its relationship with the world through perception or experience."*[34] This is to say, we are embedded in our relationship with the world.

These shifts into expanded states where we lose track of time and the analytic part of the brain thus becoming fully immersed in the present moment are not a new thing. Distinguished professor of Psychology Mihaly Csíkszentmihályi first coined them as *"flow states."* In an interview with Wired magazine, Csíkszentmihályi described flow as *"being completely involved in an activity for its own sake. The ego falls away. Time flies. Every action, movement, and thought follows inevitably from the previous*

---

[33] Stolz, S. A. (2015). Embodied learning. *Educational Philosophy and Theory*, 47(5), 474-487. doi: 10.1080/00131857.2013.879694

[34] Stolz, S. A. (2015). Embodied learning. *Educational Philosophy and Theory*, 47(5), 474-487. doi: 10.1080/00131857.2013.879694 (p.478)

one, like playing jazz. Your whole being is involved, and you're using your skills to the utmost."[35] NASA also recorded a similar phenomenon to 'flow', but what they discovered is astronauts were accessing it not through work but sheer awe. They found that numerous astronauts seeing the Earth from outer space for the first time experienced a profound feeling of oneness with all life, which they coined the 'overview effect.'[36] Frank White, who coined the term, found — with great consistency, that after experiencing the overview effect astronauts world views would change. Both their perceptions of themselves, our planet and of the future.

But we do not need to go to space to experience this depth of connection — it is all available to varying degrees within our own bodies every time we get on stage or teach.

Perhaps all we have to do is be willing to open up and relate to people authentically.

---

35   Geirland, J, (1996). "Go With The Flow". Wired Magazine, September, Issue 4.09

36   Planetary Collective. (2012, Dec 6). *The Overview Effect* [Video]. Vimeo. https://vimeo.com/55073825

From Speaking *At*,
To Connecting *With*

There are a lot of different types of speaking programs out there. Many of them are focused on teaching the outward appearance of where to stand and what to say without being embodied in it. It is based in a two dimensional world disconnected from emotion and authenticity. If we use that old fishing metaphor, instead of giving someone a fish or teaching them how to fish, the 'basic' approach to speaking is a bit like giving someone a plastic fish. Yes, it looks like the real thing, but it is not nourishing and definitely not fooling the audience.

One of my clients Nat Quirk had spoken on over 100+ stages and been on national television numerous times before she came to work with me. Having been on so many stages she was comfortable up there. After seeing me speak it awoke something inside her and she recognised that although she had been speaking on stages, she had been hiding behind a facade and a deeper connection with the audience was possible. In our time working together she accessed these parts of herself and having seen her speak afterwards was amazing. Her style feels like she is having a natural conversation with the audience. No nerves or fake masks, just her being herself and inviting everyone along on the ride. She said *"I thought speaking was about firing off information & facts and 'getting it done'. I never thought about how I could invite people in when I speak until I started working with you."* Later while rewatching Facebook videos from the previous year she noticed *"it is as if something around my eyes has completely changed."* As my students discover, speaking goes so much deeper than just the words we say, it is how we feel while we're on stage and how we make the audience feel.

There is a major difference between speaking words that simply move through someone's mind, and landing a message in the audience's bodies that ripples out into their own life. In the latter your idea becomes a living entity, it takes your idea and gives it life. The audience begins to form a new relationship to the content which begins to live within their lives just as it lived within you. It grows through them touching their family, friends, work and changes the bar of what is possible for them to achieve within this lifetime.

A woman once came to one of my speaking gigs and said, *"About a year ago my husband attended a talk you did about fear …. He came home and decided to buy a house after that. He had been sitting on this decision for years and whatever you said that night gave him the confidence to make the move."* It was not a clever bunch of words that did this, but changing his existing relationship to fear. My presentation allowed for him to take the content beyond just a new idea and feel it on a deep level so it could be useable and applicable in *his* life. This is the difference between sharing ideas and creating embodiment.

The basic principle is simple. We, the person on the stage have to take the lead and open into our presence so the audience can meet us there. This is far easier to teach in person than trying to communicate it through a book — because in person you can feel it and it goes from being an idea to a taste or flavour in your body.

7.
Principle 3: Magnetic Sensing, Adaptability & Responsiveness

One of the biggest tools to delivering goosebumps is being able to listen and respond to what the audience needs and desires. At the institute we call this magnetic sensing which can only be cultivated through the presence and relationship mentioned previously. Magnetic sensing involves listening both verbally and non-verbally to what is happening in the audience and responding accordingly. This becomes far more important than following a plan or script. Academics Langer (2010) and Bone (2018) equated the rote delivery of material as essentially *"mindless behaviour; it simply treats the Other as the same."*[37] [38]

---

[37] Bone, J. (2018). Yoga and pedagogical mindfulness in higher education. In N. Lemon & S. McDonough (Eds.), *Mindfulness in the Academy* (pp. 203-214). Retrieved from 10.1007/978-981-13-2143-6_13 (p. 211).

[38] Langer, E. J. (2000). Mindful learning. *Current Directions in Psychological Science*, 9(6), 220–223. doi: 10.1111/1467-8721.00099

Here the use of *'Other'* refers to the different audiences, or even the same audience at different times. To cultivate depth of relationship with our audience or students we must continually be relating to them as they are in the present moment.

In my interview with students they cited how often teachers would typically *"very much stick to a routine."* Beatrice observed in my teaching though, *"You change tact depending on who and what's in front of you."* The interviews suggest that through being connected and in relationship with the students I am able to redirect the content in a way that is necessary to *'hold'* their attention. Another student, Fae, also agreed with this experience adding, *"It's tangible, [...] edgy and I really enjoy feeling spontaneous"* and explained that she believes that is *"because you're reading the groups connection and energy not your own internal story."* As you are probably beginning to see, presence, relationship and magnetic sensing are all connected to each other.

In application this means that if you see the audience is getting bored with what you are saying you need to respond to that. The response could be to acknowledge boredom and inquire why it is there, or it could be to ask a question, move to a different topic etc. Many amateur speakers and college professors not having had adequate training in this area instead ignore this facet and continue speaking regardless of this lapse in engagement. It is hard to acknowledge that we may not have the rooms attention, and a little part of us panics inside and takes it personally.

This panic urges us to persevere instead of slowing down to re-establish connection.

Years ago I was speaking in Perth as part of a national speaking tour. I got sick on the first day and as my fever flared up I requested they move my slot to the last person on the lineup as I spent the day in the park recovering. On Sunday evening when it was my turn to speak the room of 200 attendees was now down to about 150 with empty chairs freckled all over the room. Over a quarter of them had probably departed because they were exhausted or sick of being sold to after two days of speaker after speaker.

As I got on stage I felt the exhaustion of the room. Peoples eyes were glazed over, shoulders slumped and there were two women in the front row playing on their phones and completely ignoring me. Great start I thought. I tried to engage the room as I would normally but they had no attention to give. I then did something I had never done before.

My heart started pounding. '*Really?* Was I *really* going to do this?' I thought. As I was questioning it I already found myself walking towards one of the empty chairs in the front row and proceeding to stand on it.

NOW touring above the room I got *EVERYONES* attention! Instantly all the eyes were on me as if thinking '*Oh, this is different! Whats happening?!?*"

As I stood on the chair I recognised that because so many people had left the venue there was lots of empty seats. I continued speaking from my now improvised soapbox while beginning to walk into the crowd walking on the abandoned chairs, using them like stepping stones. EVERYONE was captivated. I didn't even know what was going to happen next! I giggle now at how audacious I was, for this was NOT a part of me I had ever expressed publicly. I was typically quiet, shy and contained and to take a leap into something unknown was jumping into a Meta-fear experience I described earlier. But every cell of me knew that was the direction I had to go in.

The idea here is to recognise it's not about doing the action I did above, but meeting the room where it is at in the current moment, and this can only be done if you are listening with your mind and body to what is happening in the room moment to moment. For a long time the old-school method has treated audiences like passive listeners obliged to listen to anything the speaker has pre-written and rehearsed. This is not the case anymore. Audiences are living, breathing human beings and the more you engage and connect with them in a way that acknowledges this, the more they will naturally open to give you their attention.

I remember the first time I saw Dr. John Demartini on stage. He was a well established author and intellectual. The auditorium probably had 500+ seats and the stage was equally massive, at least shoulder height. As I walked into the auditorium I ran into an acquaintance who I didn't know was coming (who later also became a mentor and good friend) and we sat ourselves in the front row. We did not know any of the speakers on for that day, and I do not remember the first few speakers but I viscerally remember when Dr. Demartini came out and began speaking. This one crucial moment is still etched in my memory which both captures principle two and three of the Enlivened Method. He took the mic and walked to the *very edge* of the stage. He was so far on the edge the tips of his shiny black shoes were hanging in mid-air in front of us. From here he proceeded to deliver point after point rippling all of us with goosebumps. He did not move his cliff-hanging toes while delivering insights and wisdom firing away like a cannon, over and over again. My friend and I turned to each other repeatedly with massive spontaneous smiles exuding how powerfully his words were landing for us. He was not just on stage to give a talk. John *really* cared. He *cared* about his message, he cared about us as people, he cared about actually having us receive the depth of his message. He literally took a step beyond where any other speakers were willing to go (most just stood in the middle of the stage as if there was an invisible circle holding them there). John braved connection and adapted to the room. Where a stage that size may usually debilitate a speaker and create separation with an audience, he moved in and brought his heart to us. And we got the message. Not just with his words but through his whole body. It landed.

Changing tact in this way can be a vulnerable experience as you have to see the audience and let the audience see you. But it is ultimately very rewarding.

Some tips for developing magnetic sensing and different options for pivoting:

Pause & Breathe

Most speakers are terrified of stopping or being seen on stage, so they avoid this by either avoiding looking at the audience, or speaking really fast. Instead, if you think you may be losing the audience, stop and look at them, breathe and notice what is happening for them.

Are they engaged? Are they listening? This pause will naturally draw an audience's attention back in as you have created more space. From here you can find a genuine way to meet them and redirect the conversation.

Facts to Stories

If you have been delivering too much content try switching into a story that makes you come alive, as they will feel this too. Content is usually made up of principles, theories, stats and ideas. It tends to be more dry and doesn't activate emotion. Stories have characters and drama, they naturally captivate us, so if you can weave stories with your content you will naturally take the audience with you. Even if your content is data heavy, try to discover and tell the stories in the data.

Story to Personal Relevance

If you have been telling personal stories and the audience looks glazed over, make sure your stories are relevant to *their* lives. What are the connections? Why are you telling these stories? For example, if you tell a story about your dog dying and how it impacted you, you need to connect this to what this means to the audience. This could be saying that beyond it being your dog, we all experience loss and when we lose that which we value it allows us to appreciate life. Not everyone has had a dog, but everyone has had loss in some variety. Everything you say has to be relatable back to this specific audience, their values and it has to follow the thread of the key idea you are communicating in this talk.

Translate Technical Jargon

Technical jargon is great for establishing expertise but can also be the quickest way to lose the audience's attention. If you use technical words it is necessary to define and translate them into concepts your audience can understand. This was the seminal idea behind Ted talks and what has made them a great success. They ask experts to convey their knowledge in language that would be easily understood by someone who is not in their field of expertise. A good way to gauge this is asking yourself *"Would an intelligent 15 year old understand what I am saying?"* If not, change or explain it with as few words and as much clarity as possible. The only exception to this rule is if you are speaking to people who already have an established understanding of the technicalities. For example, talking about genomes to biologists is fine, but would be confusing at a health conference. Accordingly, all your talks should be modified based on the audience.

Asking Questions

Questions create intrigue and show your audience that you are interested in their experience during the talk. The non-verbal communication created through asking questions also allows the information and attention to move back and forth between you and the audience, which additionally creates more presence in the room. It also breaks up your dominant speaking patterns which further adds to engagement. In the Enlivened Speaking Institute *Asking Questions* is a whole module in itself where we teach the 5 different levels of questioning and how and when to apply which one. For now though, consider what are the most important questions you could ask your audience to bring them into relationship with your content?

As you begin to integrate the above you will discover the capacity to hold attention for longer periods of time and work more deeply with these levels of attention.

Recognise though that this is a process. I often tell students when they get on stage just focus on one or two things they want to apply during this talk. There is a pdf I give them on which they prep their talks, and underneath the bullet points there is a space to enter what they are focusing on while they deliver this content. This can be as simple as during this talk I'm going to focus on asking questions or having specific and clear endings to my stories that make a point. It does not have to be complicated. As we break up our habitual patterns of speaking and presenting and respond to what is happening in the room, we allow for far more life and engagement to stream through us.

A variation of this is also offered to you for free in the workbook that comes with this book.[39]

---

[39] Free Workbook download at www.enlivenedspeakinginstitute.com/bonus

8.
Falling In Love With The Process

Falling in love with the process of authenticity and connection in speaking is one of the greatest gifts I can invite you into. You won't attain mastery overnight, but you can deeply touch people even from your first step onto the stage utilising an Enlivened approach. The moment your essence opens the stage you will be touching others in unforgettable ways.

Many years ago I did a week-long retreat in the Amazon with a traditional Curandero (Shaman or plant healer). In my spare time in-between ceremonies I was reading an old yogic text. Every single chapter in the book essentially kept saying the same thing in different way — to renounce everything and come back to the true self. At one point though there was *one* single paragraph in the whole book that read something different. It read, and I paraphrase ~

"*Make enough money so you can learn from the best teachers in the world.*" I dropped the book. Everything went silent as the words echoed inside me and I burst out laughing. Was this why I had just read this whole book? For me spirituality was the epicentre of my life, and these words had just connected me to recognising that working with the masters is what I really desired, and what linked my life's work to my spiritual path.

The Gift of Mastery

When a teacher has an established level of mastery in their field they allow their students to develop a relationship to that skill in far less time. It is a shortcut for a couple of reasons, one of them is what was shared previously in the Golden Triangle and we can call osmosis, we begin to learn through embodiment. Secondly the teacher can point out to the student in real-time what they are missing or completely unaware of. We often don't know what we don't know. Have you ever tried learning something for the first time and found yourself saying, *"Whoa, there was so much more to this than I was aware of!?"*

I remember when I was in my teens I used to love snowboarding. There was something about being on the snow that made me forget about life, without having words for it at the time it was one of my favourite access points to 'flow state'. It was fun, and falling on the snow didn't hurt either — which was good as I did a lot of falling. After a couple of years as I improved I began learning how to carve. Carving is when you ride on the thin edge of the board. This means you can make turns *A LOT* faster and keep building speed while turning. After a few years of practising this, I could eventually do it with one side a lot better than the other.

The following year I went to the snow with a group of friends one of whom was my friend Shelly. She had only started snowboarding the previous year but had spent a lot of that time learning from instructors. It blew me away because she had learnt to carve in less than two years where it had taken me three to four. I was a bit angry, sad and annoyed with myself because I had worn the time of learning how to carve as some sort of badge, 'I had done it myself.' I recognised though she could do it just as well as me and having spent half as much time on the snow. While I was resentful of my stubborn attitude the experience highlighted to me the importance of studying with the best if we want to develop to our fullest potential. Time is the most valuable asset we have. The only one we can not get more of. Why spend time discovering on our own what others have already refined?

I once had someone ask, *"What if I just learn myself what you're teaching?*

Yeah, you can, but why spend over 10 years and invest over 10x the amount to do what I can teach you with a fraction of that investment. The extensiveness of my studies and immersions has included studying speaking, dance, movement, spirituality, meditation, comedy, etc. What has taken me 10 years to refine you can learn in a lot less time. Think about how much more value you will offer your audiences delivering your content in an Enlivened style that has been refined for you? It is more exciting for me to be on the cutting edge with you. To have more of us powerfully impacting people's lives and in turn discovering what's possible for human connection. Together to bring even more enlivenment and transmission into speaking, teaching and facilitating. To enable others to learn more in less time. To build new reference points for life. This is what excites me.

The Relationship To Mastery

The magic I was able to bring to the stage was done through studying the breadth of different and often unrelated modalities. This breadth allowed me to glean into what was invisible or unspoken to outsiders. For example, dance mentors I studied with taught me how to see, feel and read the body in a way public speaking teachers had no awareness of. I would never have learnt this from studying only with speakers. Dancers had different cues, observations, and methods in the way they worked with groups. This is similar to elements I have picked up from comedians, master yoga teachers, embodiment experts etc. My desire for being on the cutting edge meant that as I journeyed into these fields I would extract the essence of what was most useful and bring it back to speaking. Below are some of the major influences that I have woven into the Enlivened speaking method:

- Meditation firstly taught me how to sit in and become present.

- Yoga asana (postures) connected me to embodiment and beginning to feel the body as it's own organism.

- Yoga as a spiritual path taught me the depth of feeling that was truly possible and the wisdom of following through our soul's path.

- Speaking taught me the dynamics of range, how to ask powerful questions and the gift of selling from the stage when the attention is fully on you as the speaker.

- Academia taught me the power of rigour, research and reflection. How to clearly articulate and define the magic of my teaching practises. It humbled me to learn from the wisdom of others.

- Dance and movement teachers taught me to notice how bodies communicate through spaces silently. They used different perspectives, cues and vantage points.

- Comedy and improvisation taught me the power of being able to command laughter by knowing how to structure stories in a way where I would know exactly what word would create laughter. It taught me the value of using humour to break down resistance and create connection through play.

- Master storytellers taught me how to craft and deliver captivating stories that take audiences on an adventure with me.

Over these past ten years I have taught and presented many different topics in a vast variety of different platforms. The topics have included Public Speaking, Photography, Meditation, Sales, Team Culture, Leadership, Yoga, Sexuality, Men's Work, Relationships, etc.

Over the past two years I have had the biggest gift of all which was teaching my students and clients everything I had learnt over these past 10 years. It has allowed other leaders, speakers and teachers to apply these teachings to their stages, teams, audiences and students. To create deep heartfelt connection.

We all have a path of mastery. Mastery is where we can apply ourselves and be of service to life most fully. This relationship when nurtured, begins to flow out to all other parts of our life. Through speaking and presence I have discovered who I am as a person on and off the stage, created deeper relationships with my parents, and overcome anxieties I never thought possible. Speaking and presence have opened me up to relate to my entire life in a new way and this is not unique to just me. I see it over and over again in my students also. This is the path of the speaker.

The biggest lessons I learnt about life emerged from my relationship with the stage.

This yearning for more, for mastery, is inherent within all of us. There is a path that is here to take us home, and for many of you reading this book the path of speaking is calling to you. When we are on that path it is insatiable. This relationship to life in my opinion is perhaps best encapsulated by Henry David Thoreau when he wrote:

"*I went to the woods because I wished to live deliberately, to front only the essential facts of life, and see if I could not learn what it had to teach, and not, when I came to die, discover that I had not lived. I did not wish to live what was not life, living is so dear; nor did I wish to practise resignation, unless it was quite necessary. I wanted to live deep and suck out all the marrow of life. [...]* "[40]

Mastery is the path we chose that draws us closest to life.

May you find your mastery through speaking, teaching and facilitating.

---

[40] Thoreau, H. D. (2016). Walden. Macmillan Collector's Library. New York :Norton

9.
What Is Your Message?

Discovering Your Message

Many people think they need to have a message before they begin speaking. For years I had business coaches tell me I needed to have a clear and concise message. The problem was I could not for the life of me boil it down to anything concrete. All I knew was I wanted to speak.

Every time an event organiser would ask me, "*What do you speak about?*" my initial thought was always:

"*I don't know, give me a microphone and let's find out.*"

At the time I already had a professional media kit and a list of topics I spoke about so often I would just do what was expected and tell them the topics. But at other times when I felt cheeky I would respond with my line above and a little smile. This experience went on for years and the entire time I judged myself about it because I was told I had to have a polished and accurate list of topics before I began speaking. Unfortunately nothing I did helped me get there.

Fortunately though both my coaches and my internal judgement was wrong.

"Give me a microphone and let's find out" **was** the pathway to figuring out my message.

My path was that of a speaker and teacher, and the only way I would get closer to it was by actually speaking. It is not something that could be journaled or refined with a coach, but needed me to be out there on stages. It's like the story when they asked Michelangelo how he created such beautiful statues, he replied, *"Every block of stone has a statue inside it and it is the task of the sculptor to discover it. I saw the angel in the marble and I carved until I set him free."*[41] Our message is already within us, but it is only by being on stages that we can carve it out.

One of the massive virtues of being on stage utilising the Enlivened Method is that when all that energy and attention from the audience fills you; it begins to ignite and connect you to parts of yourself you didn't even know existed. Often

---

41 Even though this is a commonly repeated quote, there is no reputable sources attributing it to Michelangelo.

my students have said to me, *"Wow Miroslav, what I spoke about and how I articulated things on stage, I never could have done before getting on there!"*

This is my experience over and over. The stage works on us, through us, supports us, opens us, and it is our relationship to the fullness of who we can become. Through meeting her we begin to meet ourselves. She brings the magic and brilliance out of us, for the stage is our path.

We develop our message by being out there with audiences.

YOU Are The Message

Most importantly though, and really get this: Your message is *not* about the words. It is about who you are and everything you transmit when you speak. Once after a speaking gig a woman reached out to me and said:

"Miroslav I just loved your message!"

I giggled inside. Here I was being acknowledged for that elusive thing I spent years looking for. I giggled even more because I was certain that during the whole talk I had not even stated what my message was. So I asked her, *"I didn't even tell you what my message was. How did you know?"*

"You didn't have to say it" she replied, *"I could feel it."*

This is what I want for you to be able to create.

When you move from that place of alignment, presence and connection, nothing will stand in your way. People will feel your words rumbling in the earth beneath their feet. It will touch their souls.

YOU ARE HERE TO SHINE and if your path is that of a speaker, people NEED to hear your words.

Recognise that everything discussed in this book comes down to presence (self-awareness) and right-action (the courage to act with authenticity to what is in-front of us). It is through our capacity to know ourselves and be in genuine presence (first principle), that we are able to create relationship (second principle) and consequently develop the capacity of magnetic sensing for adaptability and responsiveness (third principle).

The combination of these three is what allows us to be powerful speakers and teachers continually igniting engagement and goosebumps within our students and audiences. To quote Palmer again, when he wrote, *"Technique is what teachers use until the real teacher arrives"* he could have been talking about the transition from the old-school style to the Enlivened Method. Palmer (1998) urged teachers to focus on *"Who is the self that teaches?"*[42] This is not just the soul of his message but also captures that of the Enlivened Speaking Method. It is who we are at our core, our presence that is most important. It is by knowing ourselves that we understand how to reach others and make an impact in their lives.

---

42   Palmer, P. J. (1998). *The courage to teach: exploring the inner landscape of a teacher's life.* San Francisco, CA: Jossey-Bass. (p. 7).

The Next Step

For many on the speaking path the next step forward is to start.

This could mean putting your hand up to do that speech, meeting or class you've been thinking about.

It could mean making that call to book a gig.

Or it could mean doing a program at the Enlivened Speaking Institute.

Whatever it is, make an effort to act on it now.

The biggest way to get ahead with mastering speaking and forging your way forward is to begin, and incrementally keep stepping forward.

Through the three principles outlined in this text you have all the fundamentals you need to create genuine connection every time you speak to an audience.

Additionally we know not all teaching happens through books — that's probably why *we* are *speakers*. It is one thing to understand these teachings cognitively with the mind and a different experience entirely to feel and know them in your body. I have had students study with me for years as they began to discover how deeply we can refine our levels of communication and connection with the audience. From this bodily knowing comes the ability to be able to enact and utilise these skills when you are on stage under the presence of watching eyes.

There will be many of you that feel and desire to learn and embody these teachings more deeply and have them become a regular part of your life. For that reasons we have featured the Enlivened Speaking Institutes offerings on the following page and how you can continue to work with us.

My role is to support you to bring your message to the world more deeply.

I offer you my blessings wherever your message takes you.

May you bring forth all life has offered inside of you.

The Enlivened Speaking Institute

The Enlivened Speaking Institute offers a range of programs from overcoming fear, the basics of Enlivened Speaking, to Mastery, and our immersive six month mentorship where we guide you through every step of the process.

Mastery
6-month immersive transformation

Our flagship offering, this intensive, expert-level course supports students in mastering the art of speaking and self-expression as an art of living. As you become the *living transmission* of your message and your story, you'll cultivate a deeper personal presence both on- and off-stage, and the ability to connect to people in a way that words alone can not.

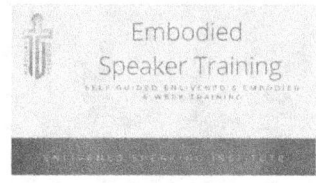

Embodied Speaker Training
6 week self-guided paradigm shift

Our intermediate training has been created to help you find courage, confidence and presence on stage. Deep and experiential, it is designed to integrate content throughout as you gently step out of your comfort zone and into your power. Successful completion will prepare students to fully engage audiences on both digital and in-person stages.

Metafear: using fear as a tool for personal evolution

2 week self-guided learning journey

In this foundational training, students are invited to deconstruct their relationship to one of our greatest inhibitors in life: fear. Through theory and practical exercises, students will become more skilled at moving *through* fear and procrastination, using these blocks as tools for transformation as you embody more spontaneity, authenticity and aliveness in your personal expression.

If you want to read more about the work we offer you can book a call with me or one of the team at:

https://calendly.com/miroslavp/discovery

Sometimes people ask, *"Why now?... What if I don't have any speaking gigs booked?"*

Well, it's like preparing for a sporting match. If you wait until match-day to begin practising, you've left it too late.

Our greatest regrets are what lays unexpressed within us.

www.enlivenedspeakinginstitute.com

Additionally I also offer speaking engagements, corporate trainings and keynotes, for which I can be contacted at **www.miroslavp.com**

References

Ayan, S. J. (2005). The will to win. Scientific American Mind, 16(1), 64–69. http://dx.doi.org/10.1038/scientificamericanmind0405-64.

Bache, C. M. (2008). The Living Classroom: Teaching And Collective Consciousness. SUNY Press.

Bone, J. (2018). Yoga and pedagogical mindfulness in higher education. In N. Lemon & S. McDonough (Eds.), Mindfulness in the Academy (pp. 203-214). Retrieved from 10.1007/978-981-13-2143-6_13

Bathmaker, A.-M., & Avis, J. (2005). Is that 'tingling feeling' enough? Constructions of teaching and learning in further education. Educational Review, 57(1), 3–20. Battista, G. (2004). The runner's high: Illumination and ecstasy in motion. New York: Breakaway Books.

Borovica, T. (2017). Dancing the strata: Investigating affective flows of moving/ dancing bodies in the exploration of bodily (un)becoming. *Qualitative Inquiry, 25*(1),

Brook, A. (2009). The potentiality of authenticity in becoming a teacher. *Educational Philosophy and Theory, 41*(1), 46-59. doi: 10.1111/j.1469-5812.2008.00474.x

Butler, E. et al. (2003). The Social Consequences of Expressive Suppression. American Psychological Association, Inc. Emotion, Vol. 3, No. 1, 48–67 doi:10.1037/1528-3542.3.1.48

Cranton, P., & Carusetta, E. (2004). Perspectives on authenticity in teaching. *Adult Education Quarterly, 55*(1), 5–22. doi: 10.1177/0741713604268894

Dewey, J. (1933). How we think. Buffalo, NY: Prometheus Books.

Dixon, M., & Senior, K. (2011). Appearing pedagogy: From embodied learning and teaching to embodied pedagogy. Pedagogy, Culture & Society, 19(3), 473-484. doi: 10.1080/14681366.2011.632514

Docan-Morgan, T., & Nelson, L. L. (2015). The benefits and necessity of public speaking education. In K. Vaidya (Ed.)

Forgasz, R. (2019). Supporting teachers' critical reflection through embodied practice of the Rainbow of Desire. *The Educational Forum,* 83(4), 401-417. doi: https://doi.org/10.1080/00131725.2019.1624904

Geirland, J, (1996). "Go With The Flow". Wired Magazine, September, Issue 4.09

Goss, P., Sonnemann, J., & Griffiths, K. (2017). Engaging students: creating classrooms that improve learning (No. 2017-01). Retrieved from https://grattan.edu.au/wp-content/uploads/2017/02/Engaging-students-creating-classrooms-that-improve-learning.pdf

Griffiths, R., Richards, W., Johnson, M., McCann, U., & Jesse, R. (2008). abstract

Gould, S. J. (1991). The self-manipulation of my pervasive, perceived vital energy through product use: An introspective-praxis perspective. Journal of Consumer Research, 18(2), 194–207.

Hufford, D. (2014). Presence in the classroom. New Directions for Teaching and Learning, 2014(140), 11-21. doi: 10.1002/tl.20109

Latta, M. M., & Buck, G. (2008). Enfleshing embodiment: 'Falling into trust' with the body's role in teaching and learning. *Educational Philosophy and Theory,* 40(2), 315-329. doi: 10.1111/j.1469-5812.2007.00333.x

Kempton, S. (2014) Doorways To The Infinite: The Art & Practise of Tantric Meditation. Sounds True.

Kerr, M. (2017). Scream: Chilling Adventures In The Science of Fear. Public Affairs.

Kreber, C. (2007). What's it really all about? The scholarship of teaching and learning as an authentic practice. *International Journal for the Scholarship of Teaching and Learning, 1*(1), 1-4. doi: http://dx.doi.org/10.20429/ijsotl.2007.010103

Langer, E. J. (2000). Mindful learning. Current Directions in Psychological Science, 9(6), 220–223. doi: 10.1111/1467-8721.00099

Lew, A. (2005). Be Still And Get Going: A Jewish Meditation Practise For Real Life. Little Brown & Company.

Maruskin, L. A., Thrash, T. M., & Elliot, A. J. (2012). The chills as a psychological construct: Content universe, factor structure, affective composition, elicitors, trait antecedents, and consequences. Journal of Personality and Social Psychology, 103(1), 135–157. http://dx.doi.org/10.1037/a0028117

Masterclass. (Publication date not offered). Steve Martin Teaches Comedy [Video]. Masterclass. https://www.masterclass.com/classes/steve-martin-teaches-comedy

Mulcahy, D. (2015). Body matters: The critical contribution of affect in school classrooms and beyond. In B. Green & N. Hopwood (Eds.), *The body in professional practice, learning and education* (pp. 105-120). Cham, Switzerland: Springer International Publishing.

Munro, M. (2018). Principles for embodied learning approaches. *South African Theatre Journal, 31*(1), 5-14. doi: 10.1080/10137548.2017.1404435

NINDS (2017). Paresthesia information page. National Institute of Neurological Disorders and Stroke. Retrieved August 13, 2021, from <https://www.ninds.nih.gov/Disorders/All-Disorders/Paresthesia-Information-Page>

O'Hair, D., Stewart, R., & Rubenstein, H. (2010). A Speakers Guidebook: Text and reference (4th ed.). New York: Bedford/St. Martins.

Palmer, P. J. (1998). The courage to teach: exploring the inner landscape of a teacher's life. San Francisco, CA: Jossey-Bass.

Planetary Collective. (2012, Dec 6). The Overview Effect [Video]. Vimeo. https://vimeo.com/55073825 (Last visited 13/7/2021).

Rodgers, C. R., & Raider-Roth, M. B. (2006). Presence in teaching. *Teachers and Teaching. 12*(3), 265-287. doi: 10.1080/13450600500467548

Rowe, M. B. (1986). Wait Time: Slowing Down May Be A Way of Speeding Up! Journal of Teacher Education, 37(1), 43–50. doi: 10.1177/002248718603700110

Stolz, S. A. (2015). Embodied learning. Educational Philosophy and Theory, 47(5), 474-487. doi: 10.1080/00131857.2013.879694

TED. (2011, Jan 4). The power of vulnerability | Brené Brown [Video]. Youtube. https://youtu.be/iCvmsMzlF7o

Thoreau, H. D. (2016). Walden. Macmillan Collector's Library. New York :Norton

Tihanyi, B. T., Ferentzi, E., Beissner, F., & Köteles, F. (2017). The neuropsychophysiology of tingling. Consciousness and Cognition, 58, 97–110. doi:10.1016/j.concog.2017.10.015

Ulinski, M., & O'Callaghan, S. A. (2002). Comparison of MBA students and employers: perceptions of the value of oral communication skills for employment. Journal of Education for Business, 77(4)

Wise, J. (2009). Extreme Fear: The Science of Your Mind In Danger. NY, USA: Palgrave Macmillan.

https://www.cnbc.com/2017/10/04/warren-buffett-says-this-one-investment-supersedes-all-others.html (Last visited 13/7/2021).

https://www.forbes.com/sites/randalllane/2017/09/20/warren-buffett-my-greatest-investing-advice-and-the-investments-everyone-should-make/?sh=159a57df593e (Last visited 13/7/2021).

www.ingramcontent.com/pod-product-compliance
Lightning Source LLC
Chambersburg PA
CBHW072004290426
44109CB00018B/2133